Texas Bad Boys

Gamblers, Gunfighters, and Grifters

J. Lee Butts

Republic of Texas Press

Library of Congress Cataloging-in-Publication Data

Butts, J. Lee (Jimmy Lee)
    Texas bad boys: gamblers, gunfighters, and grifters / J. Lee Butts.
        p.   cm.
    Includes bibliographical references and index.
    ISBN 1-55622-879-1 (pbk.)
    1. Outlaws—Texas—Biography.   2. Texas—Biography.   I. Title.

    HV6452.T4 B88   2001
    364.1'092'2764—dc21   2001051081
                                                                        CIP

© 2002, J. Lee Butts
All Rights Reserved

Printed in the United States of America

ISBN 1-55622-879-1
10 9 8 7 6 5 4 3 2 1
0110

All inquiries for volume purchases of this book should be addressed to
Wordware Publishing, Inc., at 2320 Los Rios Boulevard, Plano, Texas 75074.
Telephone inquiries may be made by calling:
(972) 423-0090

Dedication

For my wife, Carol, who continues to believe.

Contents

Contents

Chapter 6

Acknowledgments

One of the important lessons I learned from publishing my first book—the immortal *Texas Bad Girls: Hussies, Harlots, and Horse Thieves*—was that it's almost impossible to thank all those who contributed to the final result. So, thanks again to Judy Rhodes and Janie Rhodes Burton for showing me the way; Victoria Hull Jones for her enthusiasm, affection, and for single-handedly buying more copies of *Texas Bad Girls* than anyone else so far; Roxanne Blackwell Bosserman for absolutely boundless love and encouragement. Mike and Barbara Butts for continuing to cheer my feeble efforts at literary immortality. Ginnie "The Hammer" Bivona just for being Ginnie "The Hammer." The DFW Writer's Workshop and all its members for their absolutely invaluable knowledge, critique, and advice. But most of all, my wife Carol, without whom none of this, not one word, would have ever been accomplished. And last but not least, a whole sombrero of thanks to librarian/archivist Christina Stopka at the Texas Ranger Hall of Fame and Museum in Waco and her counterpart John Lovett of the Western History Collection at the University of Oklahoma library.

Preface

When this book was first proposed, Ginnie "The Hammer" Bivona, my editor with Republic of Texas Press, presented me with something of a problem. "J.B.," she said as she bit off the end of one of her Fuente Fuente Opus X cigars and propped a foot covered with a size 10 Justin Cayman crocodile cowboy boot on the open drawer of her desk, "most of the nineteenth-century Texas bad men you can write about have absolutely been done *ad nauseam*. If there's a nook, cranny, or pimple on Ben Thompson's hoary hide that hasn't been examined, it'll be hard to find."

Then she reached across her desk, plucked the genuine plastic mother of pearl backscratcher she won at the Texas State Fair last year from the impenetrable pile of rubble there, and gave herself a good working over between puffs on the stogie before going on. "So the challenge, my short, bald, but incredibly handsome friend, should you choose to accept it, will be to find some new folks to write about, or perhaps an atypical way of looking at some of our more familiar murderous brutes. Personally I've always felt that new is usually better. Hey, would you throw me that bag of Red Man there on the file cabinet?"

Well, as usual, and much to my chagrin, "The Hammer" was right. Most Texas eighth graders have heard of Sam Bass and how he got snuffed in a gunfight down at Round Rock. And they probably have grandparents over near Hico who claim the man is living right next door to them today.

Preface

The old and familiar story of Long Hair Jim Courtright's inability to come up with the required item of self-defense against Luke Short is a widely known cautionary tale of how important it once was to make every effort at keeping your pistol from getting tangled up in your long johns.

The fantasies surrounding the hanging of twenty-seven-year-old Wild Bill Longley in Giddings on October 11, 1878, sound suspiciously like they were probably started by the same people who want us to believe Jesse James, Billy the Kid, and Butch Cassidy are all still alive and living in Irving somewhere out by the mall.

Leon Metz has written as beautifully (and about as much) on the life of Old John Selman as you'd ever want to read. Other killers from the past like Clay Allison and Cullen Baker have been disinterred so often there's an absolute wonder any dirt is left on their pitiful much-abused graves.

But then, just by chance, a friend walks up and hands you everything you could ever possibly want to know about a gunman named Curg Border and the Redlands feud that made him well known in East Texas, but virtually unheard of anywhere else. Border was as famous in that area of the country as any of the other uncurried pistol packin' fuzztails who ever managed to become more celebrated simply because fate, geography, newspaper editors, and pulp fiction writers deemed one man's criminal activity more fun to read about than another's.

And while you sit in amazement at the exploits of ole Curg, you chance upon the likes of Charles "Watt" Moorman, a bushwhacking murderer, who practiced his deadly trade within spitting distance of Border, and you wonder how anyone managed to stay alive in East Texas for more than a few minutes with two men like them around.

But amazed is a word that doesn't even come close to describing the absolute flabberationism that falls on anyone who bothers to examine the life and times of psychotic serial killer and all around nice guy, John Wesley Hardin. And although his exploits have been the subject of a number of careful examinations, he is the one man who cannot be left out of any discourse about Texas's baddest boys of the nineteenth century. Because, trust me on this, someone is going to walk up to your table one day when you're signing books and tell you what an idiot they think you are for not including a man who managed to rub out fifty or more people just because he could do it.

But, hey, ol' John Wesley had some serious body count competition from his distant relative "Deacon" or "Killin'" Jim Miller. Miller might well be the more prolific shotgun packing dispatcher of men of the two, and the awful part about his murders was that almost all of them got done for money. If you had the loot, Killin' Jim would rub out anyone, anytime, any place, and in some instances for as little as three hundred dollars, and when the moon was right and the mood hit him even that might get discounted down to a hundred fifty.

John Calhoun Pinckney "Pink" Higgins' square peg might not exactly fit into the same kind of killer hole occupied by Hardin or Miller, but you wouldn't be able to prove that by asking any of those extremely dead Horrell boys. Ol' Pink was a dangerous and downright deadly man to cross even for the likes of the Horrells, and the story of his life is absolute testimony to that singular fact.

Gregorio Cortez's lyrical tale brings us into the twentieth century with an account of murder, flight, and eventual miscarriage of justice the likes of which could be acted out against the backdrop of our modern and more sophisticated society as easily as going down to the Jack In the Box for a double bacon cheeseburger.

Someone once wrote that our history is jammed with those who seemed to revel in deeds of lawlessness and that writing about those men and women on the wrong side of the dock doesn't do anything but glorify their sorry deeds. But the simple fact is that while crime is disgusting, distasteful, and sordid, bringing it out into the light of day doesn't do anything toward making those responsible into heroes. Nor does it necessarily propagate their notoriety and ill fame.

As Texans, and Americans, we seem to have some deep psychological need to try and understand those who perform deeds considered outside the realm of our limited ability to grasp. If it is true that the study of the biographies of great men and women can benefit all of us, then it must be equally accurate to say that a similar study of those considered *bad* or evil can also provide us with a blueprint on how *not* to conduct our lives.

The following six biographies are offered in that spirit. They are written with a bit more detail than usually found in efforts such as this. It is the author's hope that as you read these accounts of murder, robbery, mayhem, and death, you find yourself feeling as though a good friend just sat down with you and started telling an incredibly interesting story that pulled you along and kept you interested till the last bad boy bit the dust.

For those of you who have read *Texas Bad Girls: Hussies, Harlots, and Horse Thieves,* please be advised that this work *is* somewhat different. The effort with *Bad Girls* involved presenting as many women of questionable character as possible in the 60,000-word contracted space. In this instance the author wanted to give a bit more detailed accounting of the lives of some of our more unpleasant male outlaws and killers. This was made possible simply because the men of that era tended to have a great deal more written about them, and there exists copious amounts of information from which to glean their stories. But women of the soiled dove variety tended not to keep diaries, write their own autobiographies, or have glowingly detailed profiles written about their lives. Most were fairly secretive despite the public nature of their chosen professions and tended to simply vanish after having made a name or reputation for themselves in a certain town or area.

So sit back, relax, and get ready for the life stories of five of Texas's baddest boys, and another whose notoriety and fame rests in a simple mix-up caused by men who misunderstood the interpretation of a single word. Such misunderstandings and miscarriages have become the news of the day recently as prisoners all over the country are released right and left because misinformed juries couldn't do their jobs correctly. Gregorio Cortez y Lira is number six with a bullet in this treatise. He probably could have been in the top five but he made the mistake of killing some Anglo lawmen and inflaming all of South Texas in the process. Those fired up Texians went after him with a vengeance and ended his short career as an outlaw in record time. But before they managed to catch him, the people who wanted him in the ground most managed to turn him into a legend.

We open our five tales with the story of Watt Moorman, a cold-eyed killer who took the gentlemanly art of bushwhacking to levels not seen again until the Civil War turned massive segments of the entire country's civilian population into reprobates, thieves, murderers, and scalawags. If you look in the Webster's Dictionary under *baddest boy*, ol' Watt's name is right up there at the top of the list.

Introduction

Americans have always harbored an uncommon degree of affection for their darker natured outlaw cousins of the nineteenth century. The degree of interest and respect we tend to heap on thieves, reprobates, degenerates, pimps, gunmen, card sharks, and those our grandfathers would simply but graphically have referred to as "having his nut cross threaded," borders on the downright loopy.

All the attention to (and hunger for) information about folk possessed of such questionable character seems to have started with a flood of material by lazy writers who turned out an astonishing pile of horse fritters called dime novels that appeared after the Civil War. Most of these sorry pieces of pulp fiction tended to be long on fabricated *meller-drama* and damned short on anything like a factual retelling of actual events. (For a popular modern day equivalent, rush to your nearest grocery emporium and purchase a copy of the latest piece of tabloid trash. You'll find it squatting like a vulture over your wallet right next to the checkout stand. Be sure to read the section on space alien approval of all our most recent presidents' official conduct.)

As a direct result of this sloppy approach to mass-market nineteenth-century literature concerning the American West, men like Jesse and Frank James, William H. Bonney, the Younger, Dalton, and Clanton brothers, John Wesley Hardin, and a host of others of their ilk managed to achieve astonishingly exalted places in our shared history and memories.

Introduction

To look upon such rascals with the least degree of objectivity should reveal men who felt not the slightest compunction about stealing when they wanted and killing if necessary to get whatever they were after. Many exhibited little in the way of any ingrained sense of right or wrong. Given their criminal actions, they seemed to feel that their needs and desires far outweighed those of the stupid, knuckle dragging, pumpkin rollin' plow pushers who managed to obstruct fulfillment of their basest cravings. In addition a goodly number of these human societal weasels proved out as merely grown-up versions of the schoolyard bully. Many were just simple thugs who'd managed to master little more of life's complexities than how to thumb off a barrage of gunfire from a Colt's revolving pistol.

Often, family members and friends—especially those who chronicled the criminal behavior of such *bad men*—attempted to justify the actions of these wicked purveyors of death and destruction. They pointed out that those poor boys might well have had good reason for their exploits given brutally star crossed births into the world of death and violence that permeated the country just before, during, and for years after the Civil War. While a fairly large kernel of truth might well exist in such contorted reasoning, it must be noted that few of these men ever attempted to "toe the line" when given the chance. They usually died by the knife and pistol or spent so many years in foul prisons that upon release their aged carcasses could no longer sustain the unruly lives they lived prior to incarceration. When coupled with the fact that most of the citizens of that day and age abided by the law, attended church, raised their families, and never so much as thought of robbing a widder woman, it has to make a person wonder just what in the hell people were thinking when they set out to glorify some of those sorry, no account boils on the backside of humanity.

There can be little doubt that bad men drifted to the frontier in search of employment and better lives only to discover that their situations improved little. In most cases they got considerably worse because of an equal scarcity of work in the rougher areas on the western edges of civilization. Although the majority of such bold trail blazers found a home in the quickly growing cattle industry, as Indian fighters with the military, laborers in mining and railroad construction, or as independent entrepreneurs, a substantial number turned to thievery and murder for their livelihoods. These brigands developed a self-sustaining and hardened way of survival built on a rigorous and never ending bare-knuckled fistfight with the world in order to survive.

It should come as no surprise that the philosophical attitudes honed by outlaw experience tended to lead such thugs and felons to hold life as cheap in the extreme. This approach tended to justify the belief that the expended sweat necessary to produce a Negro or Mexican's dead body didn't count for much when you got around to carving that day's notches in the grips of your Colt's pistol. And that the only good Indian was most certainly one that could neither breathe nor breed.

The heavy hand of societal chastisement for rampant unlawful conduct during the mid to late 1800s tended to be slow at best, uncertain most of the time, and downright nonexistent at its worst. If you found yourself on the run for killing old Aunt Nellie; if you robbed a bank, stagecoach, or friendly neighborhood watering hole; if you raped, looted, burned, stomped, or knifed your neighbor, then beat him in the head for half an hour or so with an axe just for the fun of it and managed to get out of town even a few steps ahead of a posse, your chances of being caught and punished were virtually nonexistent. And if you possessed even half the good sense of any right-minded fugitive upon commission of such nefarious deeds, you immediately headed for the wilds of the Indian Nations, Dakota Territory, Montana, or *Texas*. Then you immediately changed your name to something more convenient than the offending one left behind and carried on with your life as though nothing had ever happened. And if you held to anything like the actions of most men of your sort, you went right back to the same kind of shenanigans that put you on the owl hoot trail to begin with.

The primary and most easily detectable reason that unbridled criminal activity in the American West went largely unpunished rested in the simple fact that there was a decided lack of existing communications between towns, cities, and states. It might be hard for some of the cell phone addicted folk of the New Millennium to understand, but there once was a time, in this very country, when telephones of any type did not exist. The miniature fold 'em up, strap 'em on your wrist, use 'em anywhere devices popular with everyone who has ears today hadn't yet been dreamed of in the most advanced scientific thinking or fiction of the time. Hell, as little as a century ago it could be a real problem just getting a message to your closest neighbor for midwife services when it came time for your ever lovin' spouse to deliver her fourteenth child. Prior to the late 1870s when someone stole your cattle, burned your crops, messed with your wife, or beat the bejabbers out of you just for an afternoon's entertainment, no one would rush to your rescue and slap the guilty party in irons for a speedy and decisive trial by jury.

Upon the occurrence of such errant events, if you wanted the offending villain *dealt with*, in most cases, you had to do the dirty *dealin'* yourself. Oh sure, you might be able to persuade a neighbor or nearby family member to help with such problems, but mostly people conducted themselves in much the same manner then as they do today—not my problem, don't get me involved, stay away from my house, just leave me alone.

In the October 12, 1880 edition of the Sacramento *Daily Bee*, an often-republished description of the "Bad Man from Bodie" first appeared. The writer noted some of the most obvious physical and personality traits of the universally mythologized western man who considered himself beyond the law's reach or the condemnation of society.

According to the *Bee*'s decidedly less than scientific observations, these brigands could easily be recognized initially by their unremitting profanity—in other words most sported a well-earned reputation for what upstanding Texians of goodwill would have referred to as *cussedness*. This particular trait proved especially evident anytime the bad man pulled his pistol, went to work, and sent another victim to his just or unjust reward—heavenly or otherwise. Any man who did not swear a blue streak powerful enough to singe a spinster's garters when he went "a reachin' and a grabbin'" for his hog leg was obviously not a true *bad man* but merely a pretender to the murderous throne of whatever killer enjoyed the most infamous and fleeting reputation of the moment.

Additionally a true bad man exercised uncommon prudence in virtually all other areas of his behavior. He dressed himself in the proper adornments favored by all his fellow buckers and snorters. He hid his pistol in a jacket pocket lined with a piece of oiled leather in order to facilitate the fastest possible conversion of adversaries to angelic, harp strumming status. Only upon coming together with a properly suitable nominee for graveyard visitation did he cut loose with the required string of bad man epithets—we're talking verbal communication hot enough to give Satan heartburn here—before he blasted craters the size of shot glasses in the unfortunate wrongdoer's worthless hide.

Our authority on these matters at the *Daily Bee*, who seemed to have his tongue about as firmly lodged in his cheek as a chaw of Old Stump Rot Plug Tobacco, goes a ludicrous step further by maintaining that it also wasn't unusual for these bad men to regale the soon-to-be-departed with a lengthy windy whizzer of an oration before the requisite killing took place. Our faithful observer then cites the following as an example of a typical blowhard's speech just before he cut loose with guns a blazin' and made certain grisly murder got done.

"Here I am again, a mile wide and all wool. I weigh a ton and when I walk the earth shakes. Give me room and I'll whip an army. I'm a blizzard from Bitter Creek. I can dive deeper and come up drier than any man in forty counties. I'm a sand storm mixed with a whirlwind...I was born in a powder house and raised in a gun factory. I'm bad from the bottom up and clear grit plumb through.... I'm chief of Murdertown, and I'm dry. Whose treat is it? Don't all speak at once, or I'll turn loose and scatter death and destruction full bent for the next election."

Well, it's a pretty safe bet that our friend from Sacramento's most famous newspaper never actually got himself involved in a gunfight or attempted to act the part of his overly described "Bad Man from Bodie." If he had and tried to blow off with that particular cloud of corral dust before .45 long Colt slugs started cutting holes in the air, it's a lead-pipe lock-nutted cinch he'd have been dead about half a second after he uttered the words "Here I...."

Well, anyway, during the earliest days of the nineteenth century, hosts of the baddest kind of men, most of them more awful than the fabled "Bad Man from Bodie" ever thought about being, flooded a section of East Texas referred to as the *Neutral Ground*. Spain and the United States established this buffer zone shortly after the Louisiana Purchase in an effort to avert the possibility of bloodshed between citizens of what was still Mexico and residents of America's most recently acquired piece of manifest destiny. But wouldn't you just know Murphy's Law worked full force almost two hundred years before the man was born, and no one at the time could categorically agree on any actual boundaries for the region.

In spite of this lack of bureaucratic concurrence, on November 5, 1806, a highly distinguished military commander from Mexico and his counterpart from the United States signed an agreement that declared the ill-defined area's existence whether anyone actually knew where it was or not. They saluted one another in the smartest soldierly fashion, did a stylish about face, and left everyone from the Sabine River east to the Arroyo Hondo and from the 32nd parallel of latitude south to the Gulf of Mexico on their own to make a crack, stab, or shot at just trying to stay alive and prosperous. Although the accord stipulated quite plainly that no new settlers would be allowed in the area from either side, pioneer folk from both countries immediately swarmed over the forbidden spot, built homes, opened businesses, and had kids by the houseful.

The upshot of both nations' lackadaisical attitude toward international politics—and legal boundaries in particular—turned out exactly the way any perceptive thief, killer, or scoundrel would expect. The Neutral Ground turned into a precursor of the *Indian Nations*—a similar disaster north of the Red River not brought to heel until the appearance of hanging Judge Isaac C. Parker in 1875.

All the most dreadful forms of human debris imaginable rode into the Neutral Ground on the coattails of God fearing, good folk. The brigands spent every waking moment looking for a quick and dirty way to make easy dollars off all those newly arrived pilgrims. Travel and trade in the area became about as safe as an afternoon nap on a fire ant mound. The governments of both nations ended up being obliged to send joint military forces back to the area in 1810 and 1812 to *try* and expel the numerous bands of outlaws, cutthroats, and murderers. Suffice it to say they had about as much effect on the situation as a thimble of ice water on the fires of perdition.

By 1839 the Neutral Ground now separated the three-year-old Republic of Texas from the state of Louisiana. Outlaws—virtually all of whom sported the dubious military title of colonel—swarmed over the area. A highly perceptive observer of the time noted that East Texas was gifted "with more colonels than would be sufficient to officer the combined armies of the world, even were all mankind combined into a standing army—men who never so much as killed a snowbird with a gun in all their lives." These rogues had nothing in the way of law enforcement to restrain them. The area soon became well known to killers, thieves, and cheats as a place where any man with a villainous nature, and little in the way of conscience, didn't need to worry all that much about straining his back to make a living.

Because of the confusion engendered by a constant shifting of governance over the area—brought on by Spanish indifference in the beginning and Republic of Texas inability once it had won the revolution—speculators who specialized in bogus land titles made money as fast as they could counterfeit their next certificate.

The newly formed republic tried to remedy the situation as quickly as possible by allowing for the election of local judges and a board of county commissioners who were responsible for issuing "lawful land certificates" to any man who made the "proper" claim. A petitioner was required to take an oath that he had been a citizen of Texas at the time of the Declaration of Independence, that he had in no way assisted the Mexican government during the war, that he hadn't run from the country in order to avoid service in the army during the unpleasantness—and he needed at least two witnesses to confirm the truth of this claim.

Now all that sounds pretty good on the surface. But lo and behold the devil owned a piece of land the size of Shelby County and a home as big as the Alamo in the details. When elections for these positions were held, the "colonels" voted each other into office, and it quickly became obvious to even the most casual observer that at the end of the day the corruption couldn't do anything but get a lot worse.

Those who held such beliefs were soon declared prophets of the first order. An absolute blizzard of phony land certificates once again quickly blanketed the area. Most people found it easier to play a harp with a claw hammer than boast any ability at distinguishing a genuine title from a fake one. Dealers bought and sold "headright certificates" knowing full well the documents were worth less than the highly embellished pieces of paper they'd been printed on. Original settlers with legitimate claims to their property had their homes sold from under them, and land pirates swept over the country in packs. This only served to expand the massive army of gunmen and assassins that already pervaded the population.

Eventually the residents of the west bank of the Sabine formed into two grumbling, belligerent factions. The first group was comprised of the original settlers who watched as their family lands disappeared before their very eyes. The second was the invading army of bandits with spurious military titles attached to their names that the old pioneers rightly believed were determined to steal everything in sight. Indications exist that you couldn't have found a nonpartisan with a Geiger counter. As might be expected in such situations, a single act resulted in the eruption of this festering carbuncle into open warfare and the ascension of one man at the head of a private vigilante army responsible for years of terror and death in and around the community of Shelbyville, Texas.

Chapter 1

Bushwhacker Nonpareil

Watt Moorman

In 1840 Mr. Joseph Goodbread purchased a Negro slave from
one Alfred George—who at the time was a candidate for
Shelby County sheriff. Goodbread paid for George's property
with ten headright certificates that claimed to be worth
fifty-six thousand acres of East Texas. When the transaction
took place, both men knew full well that the documents were
about as worthless as ten burlap bags of horse fritters.

Shortly after their trade the Texas Congress inaugurated an
investigation throughout the entire republic to separate the real
paper from the forgeries. Goodbread's titles naturally fell into
the latter group. Alfred George wanted the aforementioned
Negro slave—rightful goods that he had legitimately purchased—given back to him and was sorely put out when
Goodbread refused to return this valuable asset. Mr. George
even went so far as to persuade his former possession to abandon his newly acquired master and take shelter in a wooded

area near Shelbyville. He went a step further and supplied the fugitive slave with food and clothing during his leafy exile.

Goodbread, to put it mildly, was madder'n a red-eyed cow. He told everyone he met about that low-life, double-dealing, polecat's business practices in the hope of affecting George's prospects of being elevated to the heady position of sheriff in the forthcoming election. George did what any self-respecting Texian sheriff's candidate would. He went out and got himself a hired gun to take care of a quickly growing personal embarrassment.

The gunman, Charles W. Jackson, a former riverboat captain, might well have been the only man in Shelby County at the time with a *legitimate* semi-military sounding title. He had very recently escaped the clutches of Louisiana lawmen for the foul and unnatural murder of one respected Cajun merchant and the serious shooting of another. The good folk of Alexandria put a $30,000 reward on his sorry head—a considerable sum for any criminal's capture at the time.

When the good captain refused to give himself up for lawful prosecution, the citizens of Alexandria took a giant leap forward in the belligerency game, mounted a cannon on their wharf, and sent word that they would blow him out of the water at the first opportunity. Jackson angrily affixed a cannon of his own to his Red River running paddle wheeler and threatened to turn the whole of Alexandria into a pile of blackened damned charcoal briquettes.

You have to give the man credit though—he recognized a serious threat to his life and livelihood when it jumped up and got in his face. So he quickly sold his interest in the riverboat business and made an effort to stay out of sight for a while by running to New Orleans and trying to blend in with all the other killers and ruffians. But he still had a pesky little problem. That huge reward made it difficult to stay alive given the company he kept.

Finally brought to heel in Shreveport by Louisiana law enforcement types, he'd managed to escape the very real prospect of a lynching when he jumped into the Red River as his captors transported him back to the site of the alleged murder. Legend has it that he made it to the western shore of the Red minus his pants and boots, stole a horse, and headed for glorious freedom in Texas. He and his wife had lived near Shelbyville for several years when Goodbread and George started their two-man square dance and was known to harbor a festering hatred for those in the bogus land certificate business.

As so often occurred in backwoods disputes of this day and time, citizens of Shelbyville quickly chose sides in the very public argument between Goodbread and George. Captain Jackson broadcast his feelings of opposition to Mr. Goodbread's attitude in the matter to all who would listen and even sent out letters to surrounding towns in which he labeled the entire affair as shocking to the conscience of all men of good will and a deceitful sham rife with fraud.

He couldn't have been all that surprised, then, when someone took a shot at him from hiding. The bullet barely grazed one of his hands, but the message it brought proved abundantly easy to understand—stop meddling in other people's business and shut your big mouth or you might end up dead. Goodbread drove the steely point home even more forcefully with a letter to Jackson that made it as clear as a glass dinner bell that anyone who valued his interfering hide needed to keep his not-worth-a-bucket-of-spit opinions to himself.

Well, Goodbread's bellicose note just about jerked Captain Jackson's long johns into a knot somewhere up around his third spinal vertebrae and sent the former river rat to sharpenin' knives and loadin' pistols. The good captain caught the counterfeit land certificate-passing scoundrel in Shelbyville a few days later, marched up to the man, pistol in hand, and made his intentions to do murder known to anyone within hearing range of a cavalry bugle.

When an obviously agitated Goodbread protested that he had no weapon with which to defend himself, Jackson is said to have replied, "So much the better," and shot the man deader than Davy Crockett.

Charged with a run-of-the-mill street killing, Jackson posted bond of $200 and tried to go on with whatever life he had outside of shooting defenseless counterfeiters. But when the prosecution appeared to be working diligently to see him hung for what it deemed something far worse than an ordinary street fight, Jackson became alarmed. He quickly applied for a change of venue and managed to get the site of his trial moved to Panola County. The judge refused bail that time around, but Jackson's good friend Mr. George had gone and got himself elected sheriff by then. Sheriff George came up with a cock-and-bull story about an inability to house prisoners because of the dilapidated state of his jail, and he got Jackson released.

In what you'd have to admit was a brilliant stroke of tactical self-preservation, the good captain immediately formed a paramilitary group he called Regulators. His gang of gunmen developed at the speed of a ball fired from a Patterson Colt *allegedly* to rid Shelby County of the ever-growing band of outlaws, highwaymen, slave stealers, and livestock thieves rippin' through the countryside and stealin' everything that wasn't chained to a tree.

Well, anyone who believed that particular piece of blanket fuzz probably also had a box under his bed jammed full of worthless land certificates. No, the captain's actual purpose behind the Regulator gang's establishment rested in its ability to protect him from the hangman when the time came.

First thing he did as soon as everyone in the group got all his weapons loaded and sharpened was sic 'em on a friend of the very dead Mr. Goodbread named Squire Humphries. Operating under the belief that the way to stop testimony against you at a trial involved a little carefully applied force, they tied Mr. Humphries to a tanning log and beat enough of the unmitigated hell out of him to a point where he begged to be hanged. Then he admitted to horse theft and implicated everyone from Sam Houston to God almighty just to get his tormentors to stop the whipping. The Regulators turned the poor man loose but told him he just might get *regulated* some more if he didn't vacate the premises around Shelbyville and pretty damned quick. There's every indication that the bloodied but still alive gentleman went into hiding just long enough to plan out how to get a little much-deserved revenge.

The whip marks on the sorely abused Mr. Humphries' backside couldn't have had time to heal when Jackson turned his attention to other friends of Goodbread who, in his opinion, also needed some serious *regulating*. Riding at his elbow was a man soon to be recognized all over East Texas as a cold-eyed killer of a lieutenant, newly arrived from Mississippi, named Watt Moorman.

As Jackson and Moorman led their group of vigilantes to northern Shelby County, they plotted another regulated butt whuppin' for the room temperature Mr. Goodbread's old running buddies Bill and Bailey McFadden, someone called Bledsoe, and Jim Strickland, nicknamed Tiger Jim. Now why anyone would want to mess with a man with a moniker like that is beyond this writer's understanding. At that point in time when people called a man Wild Bill, Bad Bob, Deadwood Dick, or anything else that sounded the least bit fearsome, there was usually a pretty good reason for it.

Widely circulated rumors claimed that ole Tiger Jim had a habit of leaving a picture of the world's most dangerous feline as a warning sign to his enemies when they were about to have their behinds kicked till their noses bled. Upon reception of these ominous calling cards, folks tended to take the threat more than a little bit seriously. But most likely the nickname derived as much from a definite yellow cast to his cheeks than any scraps of paper left lying around after some poor East Texas goober got beaten, shot, stabbed, or robbed.

Jackson and Moorman ignored such relevant information and headed their bunch of cutthroats into northern Shelby County where Tiger Jim and the other former friends of the deceased Goodbread lived near McFadden Creek. But upon arrival the Regulators found their targets away from their frontier settlement. All the women and children were handled in the most unchivalrous manner. Then they were herded into a bunch and forced to watch as their homes got unceremoniously burned to the ground.

Suffice it to say that when Tiger Jim, the McFadden brothers, and friend Bledsoe made it back home to find their rustic estates in ashes, they were collectively mad enough to eat an anvil and spit ten-penny nails. They called a meeting of everyone in the county who'd ever even so much as claimed to have been a friend of the, by now, extremely dead Mr. Goodbread and decided it was way past time for a bit of *moderating* of that *regulating* crowd from Shelbyville.

The *Moderators* chose for their leader another fugitive killer named Edward Merchant. Merchant murdered a man in Alabama and, in the manner of Captain Jackson, fled the scene to avoid a fairly certain appointment with that skull-faced ol' bony-fingered dude braiding up a hangman's noose.

But before Merchant and his squad of anti-vigilantes could make good on loudly proclaimed threats of revenge for the Regulator bunch's fun and games with fire, Captain Jackson got called up for trial. On July 12, 1841, Merchant and Jackson both arrived at old Pulaski in Harrison County for the legal proceedings; each man was accompanied by fifty heavily armed, surly, belligerent followers who itched for a bloody fight like they were covered with brown dog ticks.

Judge John M. Hansford, a friend of Goodbread and thus a partisan of the Moderators, found himself so intimidated by the army of vigilantes, who bristled with pistols and knives, that the trial could not go forward. The next morning word got out that Judge Hansford had removed himself to Marshall rather than face Jackson's ruffians again, and the Regulators all had a good laugh at the judge's expense. As far as Hansford and his court was concerned, the case against Jackson was finished.

Tiger Jim, the McFaddens, Bledsoe, the recently butt-whipped Squire Humphries, and three of their bubbas—a gent named Boatright, Henry Strickland, brother of Tiger Jim, and a fourteen-year-old brother of the McFaddens—felt justice had been far from served. Their spies provided them with information that Captain Jackson had traveled to Logansport, Louisiana, on business and that he didn't give a rip who knew about it. The man's towering ego worked more than a little bit of overtime to help his enemies.

So, as he returned to Texas in the company of a neutral and inoffensive friend named either Lour or Lauer, the Moderator bunch hid in the trees along the road and blasted the unmitigated hell out of the two men. So many buckshot pellets riddled the bodies that Lour/Lauer died before he hit the ground at his horse's feet. Jackson held on for another twenty-four hours before death could drag him kicking and screaming to the other side.

When some cooler heads prevailed and pointed out the error of dispatching the well-liked Mr. Lour/Lauer, everyone got his worry beads out and started to question the good sense of what they'd done and what it would mean when Jackson's Regulators found out about it. Even Tiger Jim's brother, who was reputed to love a good old-fashioned bowie knife fight conducted in a circle drawn on the ground while tied to his opponent, voiced outright trembling fear of the consequences when Jackson's gang of cutthroats went on the warpath. Tiger Jim and his buddies headed for the hoped for safety of the Sabine's cane breaks and waited for the leaderless Regulators to make the next move.

News of their beloved chief's death got to the Regulators quicker'n a Texas jackalope with its tail on fire. They hastily called a meeting, vowed a heap of hellfire and brimstone on the black-hearted bastard assassins, and selected a new leader to take their fallen founder's place. Want to guess who they picked? Absolutely right my observant history dude or dudette, none other than the aforementioned sweet natured, loving, and highly respected Mr. Watt Moorman. His term as head of East Texas Regulators ushered in a whole new era of gunfights, ass whippings, home burnings, and bushwhackings unparalleled in the history of Texas and perhaps the entire country.

According to the *New Handbook of Texas,* Sophia Maghee Moorman gave birth to Charles Watt Moorman in Huntsville, Alabama, sometime in 1817. His father, Charles Hancock Moorman, settled their family in the Tuscaloosa, Alabama area at first, but moved the clan to Columbus, Mississippi, for a spell before fleeing the United States for the wilds of Texas in the aftermath of the Panic of 1837.

Financial panics during this period usually resulted as a consequence of bad banking practices. While opinions differed somewhat as to the cause of the one in 1837, many felt that the speculation in Western land led to extensive borrowing and when the government ordered that all land should be paid for in coin, huge amounts of hard money got withdrawn from circulation. Then the wheat crop failed, the bottom fell out of the cotton market, banks went under all over the world, and the depression quickly hammered the economy of the United States into the ground like a wooden tent peg. Unemployment soared, the cost of flour shot through the roof, hard-pressed folk in New York rioted, and the poor houses filled to overflowing with people who couldn't be fed.

Given the financial instability of the times, who can blame Charles Moorman for moving son Watt and his three brothers and three sisters to Texas and settling in northwest Shelby County. This area, just south of the Sabine River, later became a part of Panola County.

Watt made it to the relative safety of Texas under a black cloud of accusations involving a forged $250 bank draft passed in a store where he worked. His guilt or innocence for the alleged crime has never been established, but reluctance to hang out in Mississippi and wait for the law to get around to a trial evidently contributed heavily to the accused forger's, and his father's, decision to relocate.

The younger Moorman has been described as a tall, muscular, black-eyed, handsome, and well-educated young man, versed in both English and Latin. Sartorially he favored a military style coat and carried several single shot pistols under a heavy leather belt used to hold up a massive bowie knife. (Stories from some biographers that claim a gunfighter's skill with Colt's revolvers for Moorman seem specious on the surface. Between 1836 and 1843 the Colt's Patent Firearms Mfg. Co. of Patterson, New Jersey, produced only 2,850 revolving pistols of the Patterson variety. The possibility that Colonel Watt Moorman owned two of them borders, at the very least, on the highly questionable.) He also sported a thick walking stick, which he sometimes used to cane the hell out of his lesser enemies and, as did Robin Hood—well-known and popular outlaw of English literature—he kept a hunting horn strapped to the cantle of his saddle.

Something of the charismatic must have existed in Moorman, and it drew men to him who longed for leadership in perilous times. But another side of the outwardly pleasant young man often presented itself. Contemporaries have described him as a habitual gambler, drunk, and unrepentant debauchee of dissipated and depraved behavior given to violent fits of temper when in his cups—just the kind of general anyone would want to follow into battle. One apocryphal story accused him of shooting his own horse when he couldn't catch the spooked animal. Given his treatment of people as the warfare in Shelby County raged, the tale might just contain more than a smidgen of truth.

When freshly promoted *Colonel* Moorman replaced Charles W. Jackson as head of the Regulators, he and his other vigilantes quickly voted a warrant of death for those Moderators involved in the slaying of their recently deceased chief and the formation of a fifteen-man squadron of retribution to carry out their vengeance. These actions laid the groundwork for an unprecedented period of east Texas bloodshed, fear, and death.

Efforts to rid the region of those the Regulators deemed as *outlaws* started with Moorman at the head of his party of vigilantes when they caught up with five of the men branded as "fugitives" who topped the Regulator hit list for their part in the killing of Captain Jackson—the three McFadden brothers, the much-abused Mr. Humphries, and Bledsoe.

Near the town of Montgomery the entire bunch got trapped in a cabin where they had retreated to try and get some rest. Mr. Bledsoe got caught outside and refused to surrender. He put up a hell of a fight but was persuaded to die by way of a carefully applied double-barreled dose of buckshot. The rest of the Moderator bunch then made a serious error in judgment when they agreed to give up and return to Shelbyville for what they were told would be a "fair trial." As soon as the captives got back to town, Moorman declared, "The citizens of Shelbyville will act as your jury."

The town's population was summoned to a mass meeting, and the irregular proceedings (read kangaroo court here) in October 1841 ended with a vote of death by those in attendance. The three hundred or so ticket-holding attendees at the festivities then quickly hoofed it to the nearest clump of trees in search of a stout limb necessary to carry out their hasty sentence.

Two of the McFadden brothers, Bill and Bailey, enjoyed the mob's immediate attention. Reports exist that Bill spent his last few moments among the living flogging the mob with every oath he could lay his tongue to and ended with the ominous prediction that the Regulating bastards about to take his life would pay for their arrogance by some day wading through their own blood. Moorman's band of killers laughed as they whipped the horses from beneath their captives.

Humphries got jerked up short next. His final words included the admission that he probably deserved to die because he'd been stupid enough to stick around the county after the Regulators tied him to the tanning pole and whipped the bejabbers out of him. But, he said, he just couldn't pass up the chance to stay on and help kill Charles Jackson and possibly Watt Moorman too if the opportunity presented itself. He then told all the Regulator's within ear shot that if they intended to kill him to get at it. His captors didn't waste any time accommodating him. They snapped his neck like a rotten cottonwood limb and then turned their attention on the fourteen-year-old

Chapter 1

remaining McFadden, Rufus. But they just couldn't find it in their vengeful hearts to hang a child.

After a bit more thoughtful consideration, the lynch mob decided that if the boy would give up the Stricklands and Boatright they would pardon him for his part in the killing of Charles Jackson. The Regulators took what little Rufus could tell them, along with information provided by some of their spies, and discovered Boatright on a Louisiana farm. Moorman and his fifteen-man Regulating bodyguard jumped the fugitive in a field while he picked cotton, placed him under arrest, and fogged it back to the Texas side of the Sabine.

Somewhere along the trail back to Shelbyville, one of the Regulators—a former lawyer no less—offered Boatright his *supposed* friendship and told the man he would aid in his escape. The bogus buddy led the terrified captive away from camp for a sham discussion about his situation and urged the prisoner to run for his life. Boatright, overcome by the possibility of freedom, tearfully shook the hand of his newfound ally, hightailed it for the deeper woods, and was summarily blasted into oblivion by being shot approximately twenty times in the back. Stories exist that it was Watt Moorman's shot that killed him.

Tiger Jim and his brother managed to avoid Regulator retribution in spite of the fact that Moorman and his thugs tracked them for days and once got near enough for Watt to put a bullet in Strickland before the man could get across the river to Louisiana. Things didn't improve much for the Tiger man during his exile. He ended up in Natchitoches and got into an ear-boxing contest with one of those hot-blooded Cajuns, who tired of the dispute pretty quick and put a carefully aimed pistol ball in ole Tiger's head.

His brother, Henry, managed to stay alive a bit longer, but followed Tiger Jim to his heavenly reward after he got drunk and challenged a nonpartisan citizen named Shoemaker to a fight. Colonel Shoemaker entered a store where Strickland's drunkenness led to a dispute and scuffling match that ended when Shoemaker took his rifle by the barrel and hit Strickland a blow to the head that caused the rifle's lock to puncture his skull and lodge in the man's brain. The surprised Strickland was dead when he settled onto the store's dirt floor with the rifle sticking out of his fractured cranium.

By this point Watt and his company of bodyguards were so confident of their power that they more or less took control of Shelbyville, and Moorman assumed many of the aspects of a dictator/potentate. Inhabitants of the town treated the man and his little army with respect because they feared an unknowable retribution if they didn't and because Moorman and the Regulators had a big, dangerous finger in virtually every aspect of public affairs including selection of the grand jury. Indictments brought against Regulators—or their supporters—were easily quashed by a panel packed with men loyal to Moorman. In short order a former counterfeiting store clerk had managed to place himself above the law.

The most glaring example of his contempt for the mighty hand of established jurisprudence came when the district court convened and Judge W.B. Ochiltree took to the bench expecting that the men who participated in the McFadden lynching would be brought before the grand jury.

Moorman, offended by the prospect of having anyone— including a legitimate judge—display the audacity to question his authority, ordered his Regulators to load a cannon and train it on the courthouse. He then boldly suggested to Ochiltree that it might be best to call off that session—in the spirit of fair play and other such bull feathers.

Well, Colonel Moorman got a hell of a surprise when Judge Ochiltree jerked out a pair of his own pistols, placed them on his desk in a manner that guaranteed easy access, and bluntly ordered the sheriff to go outside and get rid of the cannon and throw anyone who interfered in the hoosegow. The Regulators hadn't foreseen such a belligerent response from the court and quickly backed off.

Ochiltree then proceeded with his grand jury meeting, and District Attorney Royal T. Wheeler brought forth the names of at least a dozen men known to have attended the McFadden necktie party. But in the end it just didn't matter. No one was indicted, because Moorman had already seen to it that about half the men sitting on the packed jury had themselves been members of the rabble that hanged the McFaddens in the first place.

At about the same time all this *Sturm und Drang* battered Moorman back and forth, he met and fell head over riding spurs in love with a handsome and much sought after lady named Helen Mar Daggett. Miss Daggett's family boasted of their Regulator sympathies, and she evidently viewed Watt Moorman as the most dashing, courageous, and gallant man in the county. Quicker'n a six-legged bobcat, Helen Daggett professed undying love for the debonair and bold Colonel Moorman.

Family and friends tried to discourage her from what they deemed a doomed relationship. But, as is still the case with most teenage infatuations, the more every authority figure in her life protested the more she wanted him.

Eventually, to Moorman's delight, Helen agreed to be married in the summer of 1843, despite the heated disapproval of her most reasonable and soon-to-be-famous brother Eph. The young Mr. Daggett, well known for his soundness of judgment, would eventually help lay out the site for a little town named Fort Worth where grateful townsfolk would name streets and schools after him.

One seemingly mythical story used to exemplify the volatility of their future relations supposedly took place during their brief courtship. On a stroll near the Moorman family farm, the young lovers are said to have come upon a crepe myrtle tree laden with heavy, fragrant blooms. To Miss Daggett's consternation Moorman pulled his huge bowie knife—an instrument of destruction about the size of a modern-day meat cleaver—and went to hacking at the defenseless plant with all the abandon of a slobbering madman. When she objected to his crazed mutilations, he turned on her and said something to the effect that if she ever thought to forget him she should return to the injured tree and remember the original damage he'd done and how time had managed to put it right.

There are indications that Moorman viewed his marriage to the lovely Miss Daggett as a political move designed to assure his place as the most powerful man in all of East Texas and, maybe—in his own mind at least—the entire republic.

Helen Daggett recognized the mistake she'd made almost immediately. In the months following his marriage, Moorman spent most of his time dodging the bullets of would-be assassins and leading the Regulators into one bushwhacking, night riding, beat-the-hell-out-of-your-neighbor raid or gunfight after another. Regulator and Moderator men hit their pillows at night not knowing whether they'd be alive for the following night's rest and revival. Just about every other day someone on one side of the question or the other was dragged from his home and beaten within an inch of his life on a variety of questionable charges. Bushwhacking became so commonplace that no one went about the countryside unarmed. Moorman personally used his thick walking stick in a number of thrashings of real or supposed enemies and managed to survive several roadside shootings arranged specifically for his benefit. His distant, almost nonexistent relationship with Helen became so shattered that she complained bitterly about the situation in her diary. In spite of the distance between them, however, she admitted that she would support his cause to the death.

The worst of the public disagreements around this point popped up between two men said to be faithful to Moorman's Regulators. Henry Runnels claimed that Samuel Hall stole some of his pigs. Hall made it pretty plain that Runnels wouldn't know the truth if it walked up and slapped him in the face and that the lying son-of-a-bitch wouldn't be able to get a notary public to certify he was alive even if a doctor was willing to testify to the truth of it. Each man loaded his pistols, kept a sharp eye over his shoulder, and looked for any opportunity to teach his sorry tormentor a lesson in life he'd have plenty of time to think over during his stay in hell.

It just so happened Runnels had a hot-tempered yahoo working for him named Stanfield who managed to run into that lowlife pig stealer Hall in Shelbyville one afternoon. The angry employee, a man of few words and lots of action, walked straight up to Hall, pulled his weapon, and shot the man d.r.t.—dead right there. Although we don't have a coroner's report, it's fairly certain that the slug that went through his skull and punched a hole the size of a man's thumb in his brain was the shot that most likely killed Sam Hall.

Stanfield—when he'd had about a second and a half or so to consider the impetuousness of what he'd done and being a man of some thoughtful judgment when it came to his own hide— jumped on a horse and headed for the relative safety of Louisiana, followed by the sheriff and a posse of angry townsmen.

Unfortunately for the murderous fugitive, he barely made it across the Sabine before being captured, dragged kicking and screaming back to civilization, and unceremoniously thrown in Shelbyville's dungeon of a jail. He pined away in captivity for a few days, then escaped, stole another horse, and headed for untamed Arkansas. But as that great philosopher Huckleberry

Finn once said, "that warn't good judgment." Several members of Hall's family caught up with him, beat the blue-eyed hell out of him, put a rope around his neck, strung him up to a tree, and left him for ravenous Arkansas wolves.

Henry Runnels must have thought the entire business had worked out pretty well on the whole. And he had to have been *muy* surprised when two heavily armed gentlemen strolled into his camp as he traveled to Shreveport on a cotton-selling trip and emptied a bucketful of buckshot into him after requesting a dipper of water to soothe their parched throats.

News of the Runnels murder sent Moorman into a fit of action. He had his men build a gallows in front of the courthouse and spread the word that it would remain standing till every man connected with the foul and unnatural killings of his friends dropped through the trap. Blame for the murder settled on two new arrivals in the area named Jamison and Wickliffe.

Watt and his fifteen bodyguards set out in hot pursuit as soon as they had definite targets in sight, and they managed to catch Mr. Jamison, drag him back to Shelbyville, and hang the man in pretty short order. Before they snapped his neck, Jamison confessed to the crime—most likely under some duress (read getting the bejabbers beat out of you here)—and claimed he'd been hired by Joseph Hall, a Dr. Todd, and John M. Bradley, a well-known sympathizer to the Moderator cause who was said to hate the very dead Mr. Runnels.

Many of the folks who had tried to maintain a degree of neutrality during this entire fiasco were mad enough to bite the head off a double-bit axe when the Regulators hanged Jamison with nothing vaguely resembling lawful due process. A sizable number threw in with the Moderators because the beatings, killings, and hangings had gone on just about long enough. They now viewed the Regulator bunch as blatantly in violation of their own originally stated purpose.

Charges, countercharges, arrests, and releases followed, but little in the way of justice even got a chance to prevail. Then the Regulators caught James Hall behind a plow in one of his fields. Moorman was said to have shot him to death before he and his followers struck out in a mad search for John Bradley.

While Moorman was preoccupied running the cane breaks and intimidating people all over the county, a third group of vigilantes formed under the leadership of Colonel James F. Cravens. They called themselves Reformers, and members of the Moderator faction flocked to join.

When Colonel Moorman and his death squad got back to town, he recognized a dicey situation when he saw it. In a stunning piece of quick thinking, he offered up a "peace" treaty in which the Regulators agreed to lay down their weapons and do no harm to those referred to as "good citizens." The Reformers accepted the terms of the treaty, and both parties signed it in July of 1844. The Reform faction's major error in the negotiations, of course, rested in the fact that they failed to get Moorman's definition of the term "good citizens."

A few days later Regulator spies brought word that John Bradley had a room at the Berry Hotel in San Augustine and was spending his evenings singing hymns and praising God at a Baptist revival meeting being held in a local Mason hall. Moorman took four heavily armed men from his squad of bodyguards and headed for San Augustine so fast it almost scorched the leaves off the trees.

Once darkness fell the Regulator leader ambled over to the Masonic hall and peeked in the window. He easily spotted Bradley in the crowd of singers and shouters but decided it wouldn't be good form to plug the man during a worship service. When all the backslapping, glad-handing, and God praising finally came to an end, Bradley stepped out of the building totally unaware death waited in the shadows.

Moorman had secreted himself behind either a post, a tree, or a long hooded cape—take your pick—and prepared to ambush Bradley as soon as his hated enemy moved away from the crowd and into the street. But the slow moving assembly wouldn't cooperate. Someone managed to block several of his initial efforts at murder, and he had to snake his arm around a man obstructing his line of fire before he managed to get off a shot. The massive slug bored into Bradley's stomach, and the mortally wounded man stumbled into the street and dropped into a rapidly spreading pool of his own blood. Screaming worshipers, who justifiably feared they might also be murdered, fell all over each other as they ran for cover. But the Baptist minister's courageous wife dropped to her knees beside the dying Bradley and prayed for the heavenly deliverance of his immortal soul.

Moorman hotfooted it back to his waiting comrades as a local law officer named A.B. Patton tried to catch up and take the killer into custody. When the Regulator leader made it to the protection of his friends, he turned on the deputy and gave every indication of his willingness to continue the bloodshed. Patton, who recognized the sound of a pistol being cocked, backed away and is reported to have said, "Colonel Moorman, I am your friend...good night."

Ol' Watt and his death squad headed back to Regulator country as fast as good horses could carry them. They fogged into a camp full of avid supporters amidst cries that, "Bradley is killed!" Celebratory gunfire and cheering were followed with a fifty-pound cake baked in a huge wash kettle by the camp cooks, and stories exist that more than two hundred Regulators surrounded the campfires to take part in the merriment.

When the summer of 1844 rolled around, a sizable segment of the population of East Texas had grown weary of the seemingly endless warfare between the Regulators and Moderators.

But if that made any difference to Watt you wouldn't have known it by his actions. Rumors began to circulate that Moorman even plotted to revolt against the Republic of Texas and that he'd formulated plans to kick General Sam Houston out of the presidential office, which he would then occupy as a kind of self-appointed dictator.

Shortly after the bold-as-brass bushwhacker attempted to form a new county government in July, he issued a writ of proscription against twenty-five prominent men living in and around Shelbyville. He labeled these enemies as "disturbers of the peace" and proclaimed that as long as they remained in the county, warfare would continue apace. The message couldn't have been any clearer—get out or die!

Highly respected Regulator residents of the area like Eph Daggett—soon to be "father of Fort Worth"—and Colonel M.T. Johnson—future founder of Johnson's Station—protested the action. They were shouted down by hotheaded radicals who sent word to Sheriff Llewelyn and Moderator leader Colonel James Cravens that they'd best beat a hot path to friendlier climes or be branded "outlaws," subject to whatever punishment Watt Moorman decided to hand down.

Well, any of the Regulators who thought Llewelyn and Cravens would just roll over like whipped dogs then slink out of town with their tails between their legs were sorely mistaken. They roused the Moderators and whipped them into a slobbering frenzy. Moorman caught wind of their actions, gathered all his Regulators, and even sent out word to surrounding counties for help. Then everyone headed for an area a few miles west of town for what seemed to be rapidly festering into the grand-daddy of all fights between the two combatant bands.

The Regulators threw up a makeshift fort around a log house just off Buena Vista road on the Beauchamp farm. Cravens moved his forces to within a few hundred yards of the fort, and on August 4, 1844, the party started with a bang. The blasting from both sides went on all day. Some were wounded and stories persist that one or two might have died in the melee. Blistering heat and lack of water eventually caused Cravens to fall back to a creek a few miles away, and during his absence from the field of battle the Regulators burned up boot leather and wore out horseshoes getting themselves away from their crude stronghold. They didn't stop running until they'd managed to put fifteen miles of East Texas woodland between themselves and Cravens' Moderators.

Moorman totally missed the action. Hell, he wasn't even there when all the shouting, shooting, spitting, and cursing at the Beauchamp farm occurred. He spent the entire time trying to raise more troops and eventually hooked up with his little army at Hilliard's Springs, in northern Shelby County, where they chopped down every tree in sight for another temporary fortification.

Cravens lay back, rolled a smoke, and waited for reinforcements. After a few days' rest and recuperation, he sent out scouts to reconnoiter and relocate his enemy. Once they ascertained Moorman's and the Regulators' position, he led his men toward the new stronghold but stopped at a rustic meetinghouse several miles away so his men could fix themselves a meal. By this point hundreds of men had rallied to each side, and more showed up by the minute.

While the Moderators ate, sentries sounded the alarm when a woman ignored the obvious situation and rode past picketed guards at breakneck speed. Cravens and his party were stunned by the realization that the rider was none other than Helen Daggett Moorman. He and his men, including most of the sentries, crowded around the agitated lady and patiently listened as she threw out a cock and bull complaint about being shot at near their camp. The Moderator leader apologized most profusely and assured her he would punish those responsible. Mrs. Moorman thanked Cravens for seeing things her way, remounted, and headed for the safety of the trees. The last posted guard could still smell the sweat from her passing horse when the Regulators opened fire on the Moderator camp from hiding places in the forest. Too late, Cravens and his men recognized the bold ruse of using Helen Daggett Moorman to divert their attention while her husband moved his men up for the attack.

During the confusion most of the Moderators did manage to scatter and vacate the area. Men on both sides became so bewildered throughout the unorganized fracas that they managed to shoot into their own ranks, and at least twelve men are said to have died in the fighting. Just when it looked like the Regulators would rub out a good many more of the Cravens party, Moorman pulled the horn from his saddle and blew retreat. Seems he'd just come into some astonishing news. Sam Houston had set up shop about twenty miles south of Shelbyville, and he was not a happy camper.

From his desk in San Augustine, the president of the republic issued the following proclamation:

> *"It having been represented to me that*
> *there exists in the county of Shelby a state of*
> *anarchy and misrule—that parties are arrayed*
> *against each other in hostile attitude contrary*
> *to law order—now, therefore, be it known, that I,*
> *Sam Houston President of the Republic of Texas,*
> *to the end that hostilities may cease and*
> *good order prevail, command all citizens engaged*
> *therein to lay down their arms, and retire to*
> *their respective homes. Given under my*
> *hand and seal.*
> *Sam Houston"*

It took the personal intervention of General Sam Houston, president of the Republic of Texas, and the advent of the Mexican-American War to bring an end to the bloody reign of Watt Moorman. (Photo courtesy of Western History Collections, University of Oklahoma Libraries)

The old statesman backed this order up with a call to the militias of four neighboring counties. The six hundred men who responded served under Travis G. Broocks, who was known as *General* Broocks for the rest of his life. He also had marshal of the republic Sandy Horton and a troop of deputies arrest a passel of folks from both the warring factions and place them in the Shelbyville jail where all were forced to make peace bonds.

Most of the Moderator group gave themselves up for arrest, but the majority of the Regulators had to be chased down, and Colonel Watt Moorman flatly refused to surrender. He sought safety in a nearby Regulator camp not far from Hilliard's Springs.

Marshal Horton wanted Moorman in custody but feared heavy-duty bloodshed if the capture was mishandled. Luckily, the morning Horton's posse happened upon the notorious Regulator, ole Watt had just spent a few hours getting himself good and oiled up with a few dippers of Old Spider Killer at a country store near his hiding place. He tried to sneak by Horton and his deputies by riding past them on the road with his hat pulled down over his face, but someone recognized him. Before Moorman could gather up half a drunken thought, he had so many shotguns trained on him that resistance didn't look all that good as an option.

Horton ordered his captive to throw down all his weapons. Watt dropped a rifle but claimed not to have any other guns on him. No one in the posse believed that fork-tongued bag of buffalo chips. Horton stepped off his mount, placed a cocked shotgun in Moorman's face, and indicated the Regulator colonel might want to reconsider the whole thing. The captured vigilante mulled the marshal's order over for about as long as it'd take to blow out a match then gave up three pistols and a bowie knife.

Authorities kept their captive under house arrest in a private home in Shelbyville. Many Regulator sympathizers bridled at the imprisonment of their hero and laid his situation off to nothing more than a simple dose of East Texas politics. Eventually he must have seen some serious handwriting on the wall, because he signed a document of cease-fire. Houston agreed to drop charges of sedition against ole Watt, but the former nightrider was immediately arrested again and charged with the murder of John Bradley. The marshal slapped him back in irons and spirited the killer off to San Augustine where considerably less in the way of friendly support for the Regulator chieftain existed.

Just about everyone in Shelby County who sympathized with the Regulators believed their hero would surely hang, but he somehow managed to make bond. Eventually all the charges against him were dropped. As he picked up his guns and left the site of his imprisonment, he informed Marshal Horton in no uncertain terms that the lawman's life wasn't worth a sack full of meadow muffins and that he should look for a much deserved killing and damned quick.

With his army disbanded and stripped of all the power he'd enjoyed only a short time previously, Moorman discovered the situation in Shelbyville had greatly changed during his absence. The various factions that had kept the county in turmoil for years were now working to live and let live, and his precipitous fall from power and prominence led to friction with his wife. Former members of the Moderators watched the couple constantly, and neither he nor Helen felt safe outside their home after the sun went down. Eventually she took their young daughter, Jenny, and left him. He immediately started a romance with the bottle that turned into an obsession and led to a rootless, drifting existence. In very short order Regulator Colonel Watt Moorman was little more than a ghost of Shelby County's most famous power broker and led a life comprised mainly of traveling from one saloon to another for his next drink.

In 1849 he lost all his hair after typhoid fever damn near killed him. His vanity led the man to purchase a bad-fitting wig that he wore for the rest of his life. At about the same time his manhood went the way of Samson's curly locks, he met and became romantically linked to a lady named Wiseman. Mrs. Wiseman showed up in his life with her own set of grumbling baggage. She'd managed to get herself involved in a little grudge match with a Dr. Burns whom she'd had arrested on an accusation of rape. When a Logansport, Louisiana jury acquitted the good doctor, Mrs. Wiseman got herself stoked up hotter than a depot stove, bought some handguns, and swore bloody revenge.

Since the lady didn't know either end of a pistol from a handsaw, she sent for East Texas's best-known gunfighter. Under the guidance of a man said to have something around a dozen notches to his credit, Mrs. Wiseman is reported to have become quite a skilled shooter. Unfortunately when she confronted the target of her hatred, she got too close to the man before drawing. He simply swatted the gun away and smacked her between the eyes with a closed fist that lit up the backs of her eyes like a fourth of July whiz-bang and stopped her clock for several minutes. The doctor was said to have been heavily armed himself at the time, but evidently he didn't want to be widely known for shooting the hell out of a woman.

Well the bad blood between Mrs. Wiseman and Burns continued unabated until February of 1850. Moorman decided to help his lady friend out by going back to his old Regulator ways. He hid in the bushes and took a shot at Dr. Burns on the west side of the Sabine, but time and typhoid fever had evidently played havoc with his aim. Dr. Burns ended up with a shattered walking stick, some splinters in his right hand, and a mind made up to put an end to the whole irritating mess at the next opportunity.

A few days later Watt sent word to Burns that he would be in Logansport shortly to settle the disagreement on his lady's behalf. Doctor Burns, who recognized a threat when he heard it, loaded his shotgun and kept an eye on the ferry.

On February 14, 1850, from the window of his office, Burns used a small telescope to check river crossings. He spotted a heavily armed and determined-looking Moorman on the ferry as it made its way back from the Texas side of the Sabine.

Burns grabbed his shotgun and got to the wharf just in time to conceal himself behind a nearby building. When the ferry landed, the famed Texas bushwhacker came ashore leading his horse and scrambled up the muddy embankment just in time to take two loads of buckshot in the head. The twin blasts knocked his wig off and blew most of the lower half of his face away.

Burns thought that was the end of the whole damned mess. Imagine the doctor's surprise when his gory target leaped to its feet pistols in hand. The grotesquely wounded gunman stumbled about for several seconds and tried to curse through a mouth that no longer existed. He staggered a few bloody steps, stumbled, fell face down into the mud, and finally died.

Court records from DeSoto, Texas, indicate Dr. Burns went to trial for the Moorman killing three months later. A jury of twelve good and true men brought back a verdict of not guilty. No doubt the notorious bushwhacker's reputation played more than a small part in the killer's acquittal.

Moorman's residual infamy also kept any local parson or padre from agreeing to preside over a funeral service. Several attempts to bury his body in various cemeteries in Shelby County led to such heated objections from local citizens that it appeared for a while the man's corpse might never get put in the ground.

Chapter 1

Legend has it that his widow, Helen, came up with a solution to the problem. She is said to have suggested that Moorman be buried on his family's farm near the tree she'd watched him mutilate years before.

The burial didn't amount to much. No preacher came forward to bless the proceedings. None of his old followers showed up to pay their last respects. Indications exist that damned few tears watered the clods used to cover his coffin. Helen and remaining family members placed a large stone over the grave, and even after remarrying she still made pilgrimages back to the gravesite in memory of her first love and the wild frontier times they shared.

Helen Mar Daggett Moorman McKee died in Fort Worth in the 1890s and rests eternally in a section of the Mount Olivet cemetery there. Visitors to the site would never guess that beneath the manicured grass, amidst the rows of peaceful monuments, lies a woman who took part in a gripping piece of Texas history when she befuddled the Moderators and led the Regulator charge at the battle of Beauchamp farm.

In 1926 Watt and Helen's daughter, Jenny, gave the original copy of the Regulator-Moderator Peace Treaty to Mary Daggett Lake. It makes up a part of Mrs. Lake's collected papers that reside in the Fort Worth Public Library.

In spite of the fact that a sizable segment of East Texas's population viewed Moorman as an unrepentant villain, descendants continued to name their young sons after the man even into the early part of the twentieth century.

The Regulator-Moderator War has the distinction of being the first—and some feel bloodiest—of Texas's great feuds. The fighting in and around Shelbyville did not end as a result of actions taken by Sam Houston or the precipitous fall from grace of Watt Moorman.

Minor skirmishes and unpleasant incidents in the fight continued for some time after both those events. In 1847 the worst of them occurred when a wedding party at the Wilkinson home ended with more than sixty guests poisoned by an arsenic-laced cake; twenty-three died. As a result, newspaper accounts credit Wilkinson as being a Moderator who wanted to rid the world of all the Regulator sympathizers he could kill for the sad passing of so many friends at one time. But by then the feud was on its last legs and couldn't be revived because every Texian of good will was now confronted with an enemy common to every one of them.

The Mexican War officially commenced with President James K. Polk's May 13, 1846 declaration of war with our neighbors to the south. Two companies of volunteers were raised in Shelby County. One under the command of Regulator M.T. Johnson and another led by his rival Moderator Alfred Truitt. Men filled the ranks pretty much along the lines of the positions they'd taken during the old feud. But when it came to the final crunch, they fought and died side by side, and the living returned home after the war as friends bonded in ways that only death and common suffering can forge.

Both groups refused Watt Moorman when he tried to enlist with them.

Chapter 2

Redlands Pistoleer

Lycurgus "Curg" Border

Almost fifty years after the Regulator-Moderator War ended, the area around San Augustine again exploded into one of the most violent and bitter blood feuds seen in the history of the state. Even as late as 1890 this region, known as The Redlands for the strip of rich red clay running through it, still had a frontier feel. Saloons and gambling halls drew young men to town from local farms and ranches for a Saturday night fling of whiskey, cards, and easily obtainable female companionship.

Traveling pooh-bahs of the green felt—called Fancy Dans—dressed themselves in derby hats, silk vests, pinch-backed coats, and extravagant striped pants for their regular visits. Cowboys and plow boys who drifted into town for a little much-deserved entertainment tended to be easy targets for those sweet-talking, flashy-dressed, limber-fingered professionals, who had not the least problem stripping any sucker available of every penny he had and then some. Those who made a living at the gaming tables traveled a circuit from San Augustine to San

Antonio to Fort Worth—a new frontier town out where the *real* West began—then back to San Augustine where those friendly, country sheep still had money and were just waiting to be sheared.

Faro, poker, whiskey, and lewd women drew visitors to town from a hundred miles away. The cardsharps and fly-by-night scalawags they attracted were the source of constant problems. Gunfire and murder tended to be routine. The sound of six-guns blasting in the streets was as common as pig tracks in the woods. Vice and violence rubbed the entire permanent populations' collective nerve ends raw and strained to the limits the natives' endurance and ability to keep lawful order.

One of the largest and most popular gambling establishments in town—built specifically to accommodate the most unruly element imaginable—stood for years on Columbia Street before burning to the ground in 1890. That popular and well-known cow country oasis sported a widely held reputation for being the absolute criminal capital of the entire area. Billiards, cards, and gambling contraptions of every type imaginable on the ground floor offered entertainment for any man willing to part with his money. Upstairs, private rooms served the kind of excitement that couldn't be purchased at the Faro table by way of private parties where *other* vices could be satisfied.

In this bubbling cauldron of cards, liquor, bordello sex, and disputes settled with gunfire, the Wall-Border feud had its violent beginnings. The young male members of these two prominent area families did not fit the mold of natural born killers. They came from pioneer stock on both sides whose families could boast of a good many beneficial accomplishments on behalf of the community at large and the political well-being of the entire area.

Unfortunately the Wall-Border boys also held to a single common belief that when it came to settling differences, rifles or pistols made everyone equal in any argument. They universally felt that handguns and knives were a dandy way of putting an end to disagreements in a fashion that guaranteed no avenue of appeal once the gun smoke cleared. Such men did as they pleased, took care of their own problems, considered it better to go down shooting than suffer at the hands of a fool, and believed the Winchester rifle—the gun that actually won the West—their best friend.

An early settler of the area, W.A. "Uncle Buck" Wall lived several miles down the Geneva road with his five sons—four of whom eventually took part in the feuding and festivities. George W., Brune, Gene, and Lopez were all involved in the fighting at one time or another. But Ney seems to have tried to stay out of the affair. Their extended family of Robertses and Tuckers could add bodies to any quickly needed army of defense. Dozens of friends and acquaintances could also be counted upon if anything wayward confronted either family.

William Border, formerly of Lincolnshire, England, lived nearby with his sons John and George. George married into the famous Broocks family and produced two sons, George and Lycurgus—nicknamed Curg. The Border boys and their cousins John, Moses, and Ben Broocks couldn't get along with the Wall bunch from the very beginning. The origins of the warfare between the two groups started early in the lives of young men taught that whatever else you did you must never give an inch to anybody.

As has been the case since the beginnings of recorded history and literature the Wall-Border fracas had its germination from tiny incidents that built up over the years like steam in a boiler. Most written versions of their story look to schoolyard friction between the boys at very young ages to lay the bedrock reasons for later events.

The Wall kids have been described as "vigorous" and the Border boys as "small for their age." What should be easily perceived from such descriptions involves schoolyard bullies and those who end up on the wrong end of the bullying. This kind of universally evil behavior probably started about a second and a half after our one-celled ancestors climbed out of the primordial ooze. It has continued unabated right into today's headlines.

Not long ago several incidents involving a much put upon youngster who got fed up and shot another child on the playground screamed from the headlines of all our news outlets—printed and electronic. Teachers, parents, talking head psychologists, and every other kind of nattering jellybean the networks could dredge up expressed complete surprise and consternation that such events could occur in our modern, placid, and overly homogenized society.

Those who've been the culprits in such brutality or who haven't been on the receiving end of the attentions of a determined and devoted tormenter cannot understand the impact it can have on the psyche. No, if you've never had your pants ripped off and your exposed crotch beaten with switches; if you've never been chased for miles by a kid your age but twice your size strapping your behind with his leather belt; if you've never been taunted, teased, embarrassed, or had your face slapped in front of a beautiful little girl you idolized, your head shaved, or your butt painted blue, then you probably won't ever understand why Curg Border likely hated the Wall boys with a rage that saturated his being to the bone.

The older all these young men got the more heated and fractious the disagreements between them became. Some believe that the constant hazing forced the smaller and less physically gifted Curg to become expert with firearms and a dangerous opponent who went for blood when the chips were down. One story exists that while still a teenager his unpolished skill as a gunfighter almost failed him when he was shot in the leg, or knee, and had to wear a heavy iron brace for the rest of his life just to be able to stand and walk. The story further indicates that his challenger, a gentleman named Wood or Woods, evidently didn't have to worry all that much about walking after the smoke cleared.

As Curg grew into manhood, his accomplishments as a gun-hawk might not have rivaled those of better-known killers like John Wesley Hardin, but he was fast enough, angry enough, and bad enough for the San Augustine area, and that's all that really counted.

Evidence indicates that rancid blood between these two clans finally pimpled up and broke loose during the election of 1894. Uncle Buck Wall and his bunch jumped on the Populist bandwagon along with all the reformers, radicals, and dirt poor. Known as a sympathizer to the Northern cause during the War of Yankee Aggression, the old man's newly adopted politics didn't sit well with most established citizens of the area. But he was a sly old bird and rode into a county commissioner's position on a People's Party tidal wave that also put son George in the San Augustine County sheriff's office.

The Border and Broocks tribes kept to the beliefs of southern Democrats in the Jeff Davis vein and felt the Populists were little more than radical Republicans who had several loose nuts on their thinker assemblies. Local political observers and innocent bystanders took a step back and realized that the campaign had most likely put the players in just the right place for bloodshed and violence—and they were right.

There are several accounts that claim to explain what caused young Curg to get into a head-butting contest with the newly elected sheriff. One involved charges that he extorted money from local farmers by way of implied threats. He was said to have told them that if they didn't come up with the required amount of insurance payment, barns could burn, pigs could die, cows might disappear, and other unnamed horrors just might befall them.

The second and most commonly held account claims he was hired by a San Augustine storekeeper named Lynch to collect bad debts from those in arrears and that his methods of persuasion didn't involve kid glove treatment. Then again it could have been a combination of both these tales. Once more it's a one from column A or one from column B kind of history item. You get to take your pick.

At any rate, Curg evidently traveled from farm to farm in the company of a black friend named Arch Price, who was said to be faster, deadlier, and quicker to fight than young master Border. Their partnership didn't sit well with a lot of people at the time. Blacks and whites just didn't mix like that, you know. Whatever the public's feelings on the subject, most of the two men's efforts seemed to involve collecting past debts from Negro tenant farmers. Given any thought at all it would seem beneficial to have a black man as part of such efforts. But after a visit to some of the sharecroppers who lived and worked on the Wall place, Uncle Buck's boys got good and puffed up and let it be known that they resented the hell out of having their people abused.

When George Wall got married, some of his father's renters followed him to work the fields of his new farm. Curg is reported to have pistol-whipped one of these men while Arch Price held everyone else at gunpoint. Border administered the alleged beating because Wall's renter couldn't come up with the requisite amount of cash to satisfy his debt.

When George got the news, he gave ten dollars to his employee and told him to pay the bill and stay away from

Lynch's store. Later the same day on the streets of San Augustine he confronted Border and informed him that he should keep off his family's property and leave his people alone. The two angry antagonists chewed around on each other for a bit longer, and the confrontation ended when Border said he'd be back whenever his job required it and stomped away.

Later—some say a few weeks, others more or less—Curg and his brother George ran across Brune and Lopez Wall on the road about three miles from town. Heated words led to shouted accusations, and angry threats finally resulted in gunfire. All four men managed to get off at least one or two shots, but spooky horses kept anyone from being injured or killed.

When the county at large heard of the shooting, some picked the side they wanted to be aligned with when the killing got going good, but most just wanted to be left alone and tried not to get caught up in the fighting. Both the testy families directly involved and their friends made a half-hearted effort to stay away from one another, and nervous supporters did everything they could to keep the warring factions apart.

By the time Uncle Buck took his seat as a county commissioner and George strolled into the sheriff's office, the patriarch of the Wall family tended to enjoy the friendship and respect of his neighbors and the residents of San Augustine in spite of his politics. His sons, however, were another thing altogether. They collectively reveled in a well-earned reputation for gambling, guns, and a bullying courage that manifested itself often on the back roads around town. They openly and often challenged others of their age to horse races, bare-knuckle fistfights, gunfights, knife-fights, and any other kind of intimidating humiliation they could think up.

Most residents of the area feared them and for very good reason—they tended to travel in a bunch and watched each other's backs. By 1896—two years after his brother became sheriff—Brune Wall had been accused of assault to do murder for the shooting of a man named Robert Watts. He pushed the man into a fight then gunned him down. But, as was the case in most such incidents, Brune got acquitted—self-defense don't you know. Two years later he was indicted again for beating the bloody bejabbers out a man named Cliff Woods in a Pecos promenade that also ended with his release.

Seemed like ol' Brune and his brother Eugene had a contest going to see who could do the most damage to his fellow man.

Gene was also indicted for murder in 1896. He went to trial for the killing, but incomplete court records no longer reveal details or the victim's name. A Peggy Williams is mentioned for her failure to appear and give testimony against him, and the case was dismissed a year later.

Two more years down the road from that homicide he shot and killed one of his own employees—a man named Johnson. Testimony indicated that the unlucky Mr. Johnson had nothing in hand to shoot back with at the time. Wall was eventually acquitted of the killing on appeal. No other way to look at it— you didn't cross the Wall boys and expect to get away with it.

Such events weren't uncommon at the time. Pistol fights that ended in a killing virtually insured the murderers would *always* claim self-defense. Under existing statutes of the day, such pleas posed little difficulty for a lawyer to prove. The twitching finger of any enemy could be interpreted as "a grabbin' fer his hog-leg." Producing a knife, sword, tomahawk, or tree limb could be used as reason enough for sending any adversary to the heavenly maker or his competition in the soul collecting business.

For most of the entire six years following the election of '94, the belligerent family groups openly jawed around each other. Occasionally they threatened unnamed bodily violence, sometimes got into pushing matches, and for the most part just generally kept the entire area around San Augustine on its guard for what everyone knew would be a blood bath when it finally broke loose.

Then in late February or early March of 1900, Sheriff Wall made an amazingly stupid personal error in judgment. He snatched up Curg Border on a somewhat nebulous charge of disorderly conduct, dragged him before a justice of the peace, threw him in jail, and refused to allow the man to make bail. Wall claimed that he took the action to keep his prisoner from "running off." This insulting lack of extended courtesy, which almost any resident of the area could depend on, sent Border into a fury of foaming-at-the-mouth indignity.

At a hearing conducted by a local justice of the peace, both families showed up in court heavily armed and fully prepared to shoot their antagonistic enemies' collective asses off. Everyone not involved with one group or the other headed for cover, and most felt sure the entire town would be in blood up to its spurs by the end of the day.

Somehow all the tooth-grinding, nail-biting, itchy-fingered adversaries managed to keep their pistols in their holsters, and the proceedings ended with little more than some fuzzy nerve ends. But newspapers ran the story and heaped more coals on the jailed man's head by broadcasting Curg's embarrassment along with the sheriff's somewhat unusual action.

By the time of his release, an angry Curg Border hit the streets madder than a teased rattlesnake. He strapped on his gun and blew through the door of the jail and onto the street as a hailstorm of seriously delivered threats peppered his nemesis. Wall simply smiled and waved, as Border jumped on his waiting horse and spurred the animal into a gallop.

During the next six weeks or so, the little crippled gun-fighter and the sheriff managed to run upon each other several times at various places around town. Rumors flew thick and fast that Border's resentment (and liquor consumption) skyrocketed after his brief stay in jail. Seems that from the day of his discharge from Sheriff Wall's lockup, Border never passed up a chance to let his enemy know that getting even for what he perceived as an assault on the family's good name had become his life's work.

In early April the two men bumped into each other for the final time. Threats got hurled in every direction again, but this time Curg Border must have had all he could take. Some accounts claim that he stomped away from the confrontation, got a shotgun from somewhere, caught up with Wall on Columbia Street, and unloaded both barrels of heavy-duty buckshot into the sheriff's back. This version of the killing goes on to claim that George Wall was so tough that being blasted at close range with a .12 gauge thunder boomer filled with buckshot didn't manage to kill him, and in addition, that he chased his cowardly back-shooting former prisoner all over half the town before he collapsed in a saloon and died at home a few days later.

If this version of the homicide is correct, it does have a tendency to make you wonder why a man with a reputation as a pistol fighter decided to use a shotgun to rub out his tormentor. Hell, maybe he just wanted to make sure he got the job done. The back-shooting part is more troublesome though because nothing else in his history up till then would lead you to believe Curg Border capable of such cowardly conduct.

Whether done with a pistol, rifle, derringer, or slingshot, George Wall assumed room temperature a day or so after the smoke cleared. His demise ended any possibility for a reasonable resolution to the long running disagreements between the two parties. Even before Wall's family could put him in the ground, open warfare became the order of the day.

Wild speculation on what might result from the shooting centered on the unknowable follow-up actions of Curg's highly respected and popular cousins, the Broocks brothers. One story about their possible complicity in the act went through the town's population like a springtime twister. It claimed that a storekeeping member of the Broocks family was responsible for handing Curg the weapon he used to kill George Wall—whatever it was. A further gossipy tale whispered over backyard clotheslines and by drunks at bars asserted that another of the Broocks brothers had bragged that ol' Curg had done "exactly what he should have." Such talk simply made the situation worse, which might have been why the tales got passed around in the first place. These stories tend to prove that anytime there's a fight you can always find folks on the fringes eggin' it on.

No matter what fears or concerns might have existed on the part of Uncle Buck and his clan concerning the unfolding events, they did everything they could to contribute to the bloody saga's eventual bottom line body count. Two weeks after George got blasted into kingdom come, on June 1, 1900, the worst of the Wall bunch, Eugene, caught Ben Broocks on the Columbia Street boardwalk just a few steps away from where the dead sheriff bit the dust. He walked up to within a few feet of the businessman, who rode into town that day expecting to attend a meeting, and put four of the five shots he fired into Broocks' chest.

Many sympathetic residents felt strongly that the very dead Ben Broocks had been suckered into a trap and murdered in cold blood. The fact that his pistol was still in its holster under his buttoned vest might have contributed some to that widely held belief.

But snuffing Ben Broocks' candle didn't come anywhere close to satisfying Eugene Wall's blood lust. He strutted all over town immediately after the shooting, crowed about the killing, and let everyone within hearing distance of a cavalry bugle know that he wanted Curg Border's cajones on a stick and wouldn't stop till he got them. You'd have thought that local law enforcement might have at least snatched him up and thrown him in jail until a hearing could be held, but there was a small obstacle to such an action.

A few days after former Sheriff Wall's untimely passing, the commissioner's court appointed his deputy, Noel Roberts, to the newly opened position and swore him in. Just so happened that Noel Roberts was Eugene Wall's nephew by marriage.

As a crowd began to gather near the jail, Eugene realized that he just might be up for a little neighborhood lynching. Ben Broocks had enjoyed the friendship of damned near everyone in town, and threats of a hemp stretching party got loudly tossed right in Gene's surprised face. He got a case of the soon-to-be-broke-necked heebie-jeebies and hightailed it for the safety of daddy's stronghold.

His nephew, *Sheriff* Noel Roberts, tried to calm the crowd by telling them he would go to the Wall enclave and put Gene under arrest. What he didn't bother to say was when he would get around to doing that and just what kind of arrest he intended to make.

The potential mob kept growing, and Sheriff Roberts finally made it out to Uncle Buck's place sometime late the next day. By then it had become abundantly clear that if he didn't do something, folks braiding the rope just might take him instead. What he had to have expected, and found, was an assembled army of at least two hundred Wall family members and friends. His Uncle Eugene let him know that he didn't feel like going back to town given the very real prospects of having his case tried in an oak tree courtroom somewhere in the woods outside town. Then members of Uncle Buck's rowdy bunch jumped up and hinted they just might go into town, burn the damned court-house to the ground, and use the coals for a celebratory barbecue.

Caught between a family rock and a Redlands hard place, short-time Sheriff Roberts did what little he could. He placed his Uncle Gene under house arrest, left him in the care of the family patriarch, and weaseled his way back to town. From the steps of his office, he informed the still waiting and getting angrier by the minute mob what he saw and the actions he'd taken. The crowd heaped a sombrero full of abuse on the good sheriff and immediately fell to planning a defense against what they believed would be an organized raid by an army of irate Wall partisans bent on death and destruction.

Sheriff Roberts, who by now must have feared the worst kind of bloodshed, including his own, went to an experienced officer of the court—Constable John Matthews—for help and counsel. Matthews didn't have any more luck than the sheriff at calming the rabble. He suggested they wire the governor. The following day Judge Tom Davis hit town and tried to help restore order. Since he had even less luck than the constable, he, Matthews, and the sheriff wired the capital and begged for a company of militia. Governor Sayers promptly responded that all the help they could possibly need was on its way.

While all these events played out in San Augustine, Ben Broocks' remaining brothers, John and M.L., and Curg Border—who'd made bail for the killing of George Wall—were out of town on business. Once news of Ben's death caught up with them, they all got back at about the same time during the early morning hours of June 4.

The Broocks brothers met up with Curg, talked a bit, and immediately headed for their father's home where Ben lay in state. Border headed for his favorite watering hole, the Knight and Teel Saloon. The bat wing doors had barely slapped his behind when he ran into two angry on-the-way-to-being-real-drunk friends, Lum Crouch and Frank Sharp.

At that time you could stand in the Knight and Teel's front door, which was across Columbia Street from the courthouse, and see directly into the sheriff's office. On several occasions witnesses are said to have spotted Curg and his bellicose fiends as they strolled out of the saloon, stood on the boardwalk, stared into the crystal clear windows of the sheriff's office, and tapped the butts of their pistols with itchy fingers.

News of Curg Border's arrival at the Knight and Teel shot around town like the blast from a splash of coal oil dumped on a fire in a wood-burning stove. Whispering crowds gathered on both ends of Columbia. Businesses all up and down either side of the street closed. Officials of the court left their offices and hurried away to the hoped for safety of their homes.

The hard-pressed sheriff heard about the return of his predecessor's killer and tapped some close members of his own family for support in case things got out of hand. He, his brother Sidney, and an uncle named Felix made their way to the sheriff's office that morning and entered through a side door of the courthouse in what would appear to be an effort at concealment of their activities. For reasons we'll probably never understand, after all the stealth of their arrival, Sid Roberts went directly to the front door of the sheriff's office—shotgun in hand—and stepped onto the boardwalk outside.

In a statement for the *Nacogdoches Sentinel* dated three days later, Sheriff Roberts said the shooting started when "words" passed between his brother and members of the Border faction who loitered in the doorway of the Knight and Teel. The "words" were probably something along the lines of "there'll be a new face in hell for breakfast tomorrow morning." As the sheriff joined his brother on the boardwalk to check out the cuss fight, Lum Crouch, Frank Sharp, and Curg Border retreated into the saloon behind a wall of drawn pistols and cocked rifles.

By the time Noel Roberts stopped next to his brother and blinked twice, the Border bunch cut loose with a thunderous barrage of blue whistlers. Sid sent loads from both barrels of his shotgun to answer the indignity. But as he turned and tried for the safety of the office doorway, he bumped into Noel, and another volley of gunfire knocked him to the jail's floor and ended his life so fast he didn't even get a chance to light a shuck for the pearly gates.

While Sid bled out staring at dust devils in the corner, his Uncle Felix ran to a window to see what in the blue-eyed hell was going on. He arrived just in time for a well-placed rifle shot that turned a plate glass window into a pile of sparkling shards and drilled a sizable hole in his brain. By that point the gun smoke looked like a fog bank rolling along the Red River on a spring morning and the jailhouse's façade had more holes in it than granny's flour sifter.

The sheriff, who claimed not to be armed when the blood-letting started, picked himself up, stumbled to his weapons rack, grabbed a Winchester rifle, and took a position near the window where his poor ol' Uncle Felix lay staring at the ceiling with dead eyes. Every gun on the other side of the street turned his direction. In a matter of seconds a bullet blew away a piece of his left hand and a well-placed shotgun blast peppered his left arm and chin.

It must have been about the time the blood from his wounds saturated the front of his shirt that Sheriff Roberts recognized the difficulty of the untenable situation confronting him. He ran for the door, made it outside, and mounted his horse. A deafening volley of gunfire from the opposition chewed holes in the air all around him, and conflicting stories say he was hit several more times—or maybe not.

Anyway, the seriously desperate man jumped from his mount, scrambled back into the courthouse, and made it to the office of a county judge named Rhote—the only other person bold enough to still be in the building. He barricaded himself behind a pile of law books and had the judge lock the heavy door on his way out. The horrified adjudicator then headed anyplace in Texas where no one was shooting in his direction.

Curg and his friends stormed the courthouse and spent more than a little effort trying to break down the door of Judge Rhote's office. It must have been some sturdy wood to say the least. Their efforts got them nowhere. So they went whooping it over to the hardware store in search of the tools necessary to break it down.

While the mob was preoccupied with their primitive locksmith work, some of Sheriff Roberts' relatives, Dr. Felix Tucker and the Reverend Mr. Crockett, arrived on the scene, crept inside, and coaxed their terrified relation to let them in. They persuaded the wounded sheriff to make another attempt at escape by pointing out that if he didn't, he would most likely be shot, stabbed, lynched, and set on fire. The man must have seen the practicality of their advice, because he headed for his horse again as fast as his wounds would allow. But the animal spooked, pulled the hitch rope tight, and made it impossible for the over-anxious lawman to release him.

As Roberts fought a losing battle with his jumpy horse, Border and the mob surged back into the courthouse carrying all the tools and instruments of destruction they needed to chop down Judge Rhote's stubborn door.

Roberts heard them enter the building, dropped his efforts to get the reins loose, and ran for his life. Two blocks from the courthouse he jumped into a ditch full of water and waited for things to calm down a bit. Sometime later he managed to make it to the home of the previously mentioned Dr. Tucker for treatment of his painful wounds.

The good doctor's wife recognized the peril of her situation immediately, feared for the safety of her family, and sent her sons to purchase some shotgun shells with heavier loads than those she had at hand. The town suffered from such turmoil and uproar that storekeepers refused to sell the ammunition to the boys, and they came back with nothing. Their resourceful mother took what she had and replaced bird shot with slugs made from chopped up fish line sinkers. She intended that anyone who wanted to break down her door would find it necessary to pay a heavy price for such unwelcome entry.

Well, by the time the sun went down Border and his friends had managed to locate the wounded sheriff but weren't inclined to challenge Mrs. Tucker and her homemade buckshot loads. Noel Roberts' fiancée, Lily Sharp, arrived on the scene, pulled a pistol on the men guarding the Tucker's house, and made it clear she'd shoot hell out of the first man who tried to stop her from getting to her soon-to-be hubby. In those bygone days the man didn't live who would have been so unchivalrous as to challenge her or try to stop her from doing as she pleased.

After she saw to the care of her wounded lover, Miss Lily discovered the dangerously low level of ammunition in the barricaded home. Having demonstrated a total lack of fear when it came to Curg Border and his friends, she hoofed it to the San Augustine Drug Company a few blocks from the Tucker place. A surly clerk also refused to sell her the shotgun shells. She simply whipped out her pistol again, pushed him aside, and took what she needed. Bold woman that one, described by friends years later as refined, cultured, and willing to stand toe to toe with any or all the troublemaking brutes who'd put several ounces of lead in her betrothed.

The day after all the gunfire and dying, Sheriff W. J. Campbell of Nacogdoches arrived and took Sheriff Roberts back to the safety of his town for a sorely needed period of rest and recovery. San Augustine's wounded lawman remained in Campbell's home for over a month. Until the day he went to that great lawman's office in the sky, Campbell maintained that Curg Border likely pulled the trigger on both the men who died during the mêlée and felt sure Border was responsible for at least some of the lead that found its way into Noel Roberts' hide.

The rangers and a company of militia from Nacogdoches—called the Stone Fort Rifles—stormed into town within a week of the Border-Wall dance. The bottom line on the entire series of shootings, killings, arguments, and intimidations was that everyone went to trial, everyone got acquitted, and everyone went back home just as mad as they were before all the events of that bloody few weeks.

Things clicked along for a little over a year with no trouble between the two warring factions. This period of false peace and quiet was directly attributable to the fact that so many of them were in jail awaiting the trials that eventually resulted in all their releases. But as sure as hens can't lay square eggs, somebody else was destined to die, and it turned out to be the best liked of the Wall boys, Lopez.

By way of their collective arrogance, belligerence, and willingness to do murder, the Wall family had managed to dig themselves so far into debt something had to be done. They owed a mountain of money in lawyer's fees and associated expenses as a result of their completed or upcoming individual trials. So much money, in fact, that Uncle Buck decided on a cattle drive to Nacogdoches in an effort to alleviate some of their liabilities.

The drive led by Lopez—believed by observers the most inoffensive and amiable of the Wall bunch—started Sunday

June 9, 1900. The next day near Mount Nebo, a short distance from the Wall family compound, shots from the woods punched several shafts of daylight through Pez Wall, knocked him from the saddle, and tore his ticket for a trip to eternity. Investigations revealed the possibility of two shooters, but no one was ever charged or arrested.

Several weeks later the court acquitted Eugene for the murder of Ben Broocks. As soon as Gene strolled triumphantly out of the courthouse, he became a living example of a real "dead man walking."

By that point brother Brune had seen the handwriting on the wall (so to speak) and headed out for the safety of Oklahoma. He tried to get his father to go with him, but the old man just couldn't leave the place where he'd spent most of his life.

After his trial and acquittal, Eugene and his wife, Ida, moved to the town of Geneva about twenty miles east of San Augustine in an effort to lie low and stay out of trouble. But Ida became ill during a visit with Uncle Buck, and her husband made a trip back to the home place when she sent for him. They spent a few days together, but her illness kept her from going back to Geneva with him when he decided to leave.

A short piece from his father's home, Wall passed the Roberts' family graveyard near the little church at Chapel Hill. Rifle fire from the cemetery blew ol' Gene from the saddle and killed him deader than a rotten tree stump. Uncle Buck stood on his front porch and heard the shots that took his son's life. The old man grabbed a weapon and arrived at the scene while the deadly gun smoke still drifted in the breeze. He darted from tree to gravestone to bush in a frantic search for his son's killer, but those responsible had vanished.

Investigators found several spent Winchester .44-.40 shell casings behind a headstone near the road, but as was the case in all the other such bushwhacking incidents in the past, no one was ever arrested for the crime. Not long after Gene bit the dust and got planted, Uncle Buck packed up and moved to Oklahoma to live out the rest of his life near his only remaining son.

Gossip about responsibility for Gene Wall's murder lined up on several men associated with the Border bunch—including Curg's friend and associate Arch Price—but it didn't take too much use of the old thinker mechanism for most to recognize that whoever punched the Wall boy's tickets was a damned fine shot. Backyard gossips and booze hall philosophers all agreed Curg Border was the only one of his crew with the skills necessary to deliver deadly fire accurate enough to hit a man at such distances as he bounced along on a horse.

After Curg was acquitted for the murder of Sheriff George Wall, the citizens of San Augustine gave him all the elbowroom he could possibly have wanted. John Matthews, the former constable, served as sheriff at the time. Both men made serious efforts to stay away from one another.

But then in 1902 Border decided he wanted John Matthews' job. He managed to get himself elected sheriff in November of that year. His campaign and election went against everything law-abiding citizens of the community believed, but they were unable to put up a contender strong enough to stop him. Border waltzed into the sheriff's office in January of 1903 on a tidal wave of voter apathy.

The election of what many believed was the county's last bad man sent the good folks of San Augustine into a frenzy of effort to have him removed from office. It took almost exactly a year, but his commission was suspended on March 3, 1904, for gambling, public intoxication, and several other offenses. The highly respected Sneed Noble was appointed to fill the office until the next regular election.

As could have been easily predicted by the worst prophet on the planet, Curg Border flew into a rage. Then, he made the mistake of letting his mouth overload his backside and sent word to Noble that the new sheriff's next appointment just might be with the devil.

These intemperate jawings continued until the morning of May 7, 1904. In the company of his sister Cora and friend Arch Price, Border rode into town, got good and drunk, and persisted with loud, hotheaded threats. As the trio left for home and made their way down Columbia—where they would have to pass within a few yards of the sheriff's office—Sneed Noble stepped into the street and informed Border that he was under arrest for carrying a gun without authority. Border pulled his horse a few steps ahead of the others in his party and essentially told the sheriff that he could take his arrest, fold it five ways, and put it where the sun didn't shine.

Both men went for their guns at the same time. Noble turned out the better shot. He put one in Border's head just below the hat line. San Augustine's famed pistoleer hit the dusty street deader than a bag of horse fritters.

But, my sweet lord, even that wasn't the end of it. Five years later his two backups that day—Cora and his old friend Arch Price—got into a deadly disagreement about money. Price had been living off Cora ever since Curg's demise. When monetary difficulties forced her to take him off the family payroll, the man went nuts and threatened to lie in court about Cora's nonexistent part in an arson case for which most people believed him responsible. He caught her at home alone one day and demanded a hundred dollars for his silence. A black man confronting a white woman at that point in history didn't rank way up there with any of the better ideas he could have had. Cora went directly to her bedroom, picked up her pistol, and fired through the window where Price waited. Her first shot hit him in the mouth and exited through a hole the size of a shot glass in his neck. He staggered in the general direction of where his horse was hitched then fell and died in the dusty red middle of Milam Street.

Elisha Roberts, Cora's son, and her husband at the time, Doc Parker, both tried to take responsibility for the killing. She wouldn't hear of it and went to trial after being indicted for the murder. Surprise, surprise—the jury came back with a verdict of not guilty by reason of self-defense. Hell, if it always worked for the men, it had to work for any woman bold enough to follow in their footsteps.

With the death of Arch Price, and Cora Border Parker's acquittal, Curg Border's Great Redlands Feud finally sputtered to its bloody end.

The lethal events described in this chapter occurred barely a hundred years ago. The modern mind rebels when confronted with such unconcealed hatred and brutality. We tend to consider our up-to-the-minute selves so much brighter, better educated, refined, and worldly than those poor bumpkins who settled their disagreements by killing one another in gunfights.

Then we pick up the most recent edition of our local version of the *Daily Blood and Guts* broadside. There, we are confronted with crimes just as dreadful and in many cases less understandable, because the people who committed them often do not know or have any connection to those they brutally kill. The simple and inescapable fact such stories force us to confront is that no matter how far we might think we have advanced along the evolutionary scale, disturbed and evil people still walk among us and always will.

Our veneer of placid vulnerability is extremely thin. Sometimes the violent that sit beside us at a local restaurant while we munch our tacos, rant at us from the roadside, or go on a loud, vulgar rip in a minimum wage clerk's face, still manage to tear the wrapper off and expose that raw, angry beast hiding in all of us.

Distinct from our ignorant cousins of the recent past like Curg Border, we often endure abuse that those men and women wouldn't have put up with for a New York minute. We grovel and beg to be left alone, our mantra repeated in every prayer—not my problem, stay out of my yard, get out of my face, please leave me alone. Sometimes it works. Sometimes it doesn't. The betting line would be pretty good that an awful lot of people right now would give just about anything if they could solve their problems as simply and directly as men like Watt Moorman and Lycurgus "Curg" Border.

Chapter 3

Texas's Original Serial Murderer!

John Wesley Hardin

Any book about the lives of the most notorious bad men who ever walked the dusty streets of frontier Texas that didn't include a chapter on John Wesley Hardin would most likely be met with a barrage of jeers. His brief and violent career as a dangerous and determined murderer could easily be the modern paradigm for virtually every bad man who ever made an appearance in the fictional literature about our early frontier, or the films that tend to glorify it. Because of his singular position in the starry heavens of mass killers, his life will be examined in somewhat more detail than others included in our collection of bad boy biographies.

In Bill O'Neal's fabulous *Encyclopedia of Western Gunfighters*, Hardin enjoys the rather dubious position of number two with a bullet in the overall gunfighter statistic of killings that can unquestionably be attributed directly to his name. Somewhat more impressive is the fact that he was undeniably involved in almost twice as many gunfights as the leader of this bloody pack, a distant cousin called Killin' Jim Miller. And, for those who really want to be impressed, Hardin managed to achieve these heady levels of death and destruction during a brief nine-year period between 1868 and his incarceration for murder in 1877 at the tender age of twenty-five. All you have to do is crunch the numbers and you'll easily detect that he left all this butchery in his wake starting around fourteen or fifteen years of age! There can be very little doubt about it; Hardin was definitely a murderer of the *serial* type.

Since about 1970 we Americans have become more and more aware of this serial murderer phenomenon. In spite of the fact that any given person's chances of coming into contact with one of these monsters are virtually nonexistent, huge segments of the population can now offer up a reasonably accurate description of them because the wicked brutes are given so much time and space in our print and electronic media.

As has been typical with almost every generation of the past, we've fallen into that old trap of thinking that ours is the only age gifted with intelligence enough to understand these soulless killers. Such men (for nearly all serial murderers are male) randomly choose their victims and continue to slaughter people until they are stopped. Most of the dead they leave behind have never met their killer prior to being slaughtered, and those responsible for these atrocities move so often that independent law enforcement agencies find it virtually impossible to catch them.

Knowledge of such basic facts and use of a working definition derived from them—*serial murderer: a killer who dispatches his victims one at a time in a series till caught*—easily constitute a description of John Wesley Hardin's actions that fits like feathers on a duck.

According to his own count, he could easily have carved at least fifty notches in the grips of his pistols and perhaps more.

The figure from other source authorities numbers the unhappy dead at anywhere from eleven to thirty. But even if it was only eleven, that's six more than the Son of Sam, David Berkowitz, a slayer of people made famous by the hysterical New York electronic media.

For dyed-in-the-wool students of the American frontier of the late nineteenth and early twentieth centuries, Hardin's story is a familiar one that talented writers have examined often and at great length. If you count yourself among either of these groups, be forewarned that nothing of the new or stunningly revealing in the way of facts can be found in the following pages. If you don't include yourself in either of those groups, read on. It'll be fun.

James G. Hardin migrated to Texas from Tennessee in 1841 upon grant of 320 acres of land in Liberty County. At the time, he worked in the soul-saving business and felt Texans were steeped in sin and needed immediate redemption. In early 1847 he met his future wife, Elizabeth, through a friend, her father, Dr. William Dixon.

The star-crossed parents of John Wesley Hardin committed matrimony on May 19, 1847, in Navarro County. James was twenty-four years old at the time, Elizabeth barely twenty. Their first child died the day it was born. John Wesley entered the world third in a string of what would eventually end at ten children.

Rumors that he popped out on May 26, 1853, with a pistol in each hand have been greatly exaggerated. His parents, both devout Methodists, named their son for the founder of their particular brand of faith in the hope that the boy would follow in the pious and upright footsteps of that renowned English clergyman. Did they get a surprise or what?

The earliest indication that something just might be amiss in John's lump of head filler and that he possessed a distinct lack of control over his short-fused temper appeared at about age fourteen, in 1867. At the time Hardin attended school and vied for the affections of a young lady named Sally with classmate Charles Sloter. Sloter accused Hardin of being a bully and of writing vulgar poems on the blackboard that brought the lovely Sal's virtue into question. John Wesley took the insult to Sal personally, heaped blame for the questionable verses back on Sloter, and physically confronted the source of the scurrilous and unfounded allegations against his family's good name.

Sloter slapped his adversary so hard the wax popped out of the angry Hardin's ears, then he pulled a knife—an action most likely designed to do little more than threaten his opponent. John Wesley whipped out his own pocket skewer and poked several large, bloody holes in Sloter's back and chest. The wounded boy damn near died. Such were the beginnings of a single individual's career of unparalleled mayhem and homicide.

About a year later, in November 1868, Hardin visited with an uncle who lived in Polk County. John's cousin Barnett Jones arranged a wrestling match between the two boys and a former slave named Major "Mage" Holshousen. Two against one hardly seems fair, but Mage probably enjoyed the local honor and reputation as the most accomplished wrestler in the area.

Hardin later claimed that he and his cousin threw the freedman twice, and that the second fall also resulted in Mage's face being lacerated and bloodied. An incensed Mage went for a gun, threatened to kill both boys (who had by that time gone into hiding), and let it be known that he especially wanted a piece of young Mr. Hardin's hide for the indignity he'd suffered.

Some historians point out that it's just as likely Mage won both matches and that Hardin acted the offended part. Given the pattern of the icy murderer's later behavior in the area of man killing, this seems more than just a little possible.

Anyway, the next day John Wesley started for home. He claimed to have tried to avoid contact with the still irate Mage and took a back way. By *accident* he ran into his belligerent adversary on the trail. They argued again. Mage grabbed the reins of Hardin's horse, and, as Hardin later told it, "I shot him till he turned them loose."

The murderous weapon of choice for the fifteen- or sixteen-year-old boy was an 1860 Army model Colt .44 cap-and-ball pistol. Those two-and-a-half-pound equalizers might well be the most aesthetically beautiful handguns Colt Firearms ever produced. Hardin favored them in his early fun and games above all others. Being shot five times at close range with one of the black powder pistols virtually assured that if your name just happened to be "Mage" you would soon be wrestling for Jesus in that great grunt and grapple ring in the sky.

There had been a time—and it would come again—when the shooting of a black man would have gone virtually unnoticed and no white man would have worried about any consequences for the killing. But Reconstruction pen pushers in the Texas Freedman's Bureau took a dim view of such murders. After Hardin fled to his brother's home twenty-five miles north of Sumpter in Trinity County, they sent three soldiers from the Sixth Cavalry to corral the hot-tempered young stallion and bring him in for what would probably have worked out to be a reasonably fair trial, picnic on the courthouse lawn, and very quick hanging.

Rather than just run for the bushes, briars, and parts unknown, Hardin did what any self-respecting neophyte bushwhacker and future multiple murderer of the first water would be expected to do. He loaded up all his smoke poles and hid himself near a creek where the Union troopers had to pass. As those unsuspecting boys in Yankee blue waded their animals into the water, he stood with a shotgun in hand and blasted the two white soldiers dogging his trail. His remaining tormentor, a terrified black private, tried to escape. But John Wesley caught him, and in the ensuing exchange of gunfire he managed to end that day with his forth killing in little more than two weeks.

Later, in his autobiography, Hardin said he demanded of the last man executed that he surrender himself in the "name of the Confederacy." His rather odd request was proffered while his horrified prey fired several defensive shots in the young killer's direction, one of which put a painful but superficial hole in the boy assassin's left arm. John Wesley's endless supply of willing friends helped him conceal the bodies. Then he hotfooted it for the wilds of Pisga Ridge where his Aunt Susanna Anderson ran a school and needed a teacher of his talent, intelligence, and good-natured disposition.

But keeping class must have been pretty tame stuff after you've shot the bejabbers out of four grown men and felt the power an act of such magnitude must bring to those who seek it. Little more than three months after his career as a school-teacher started, it abruptly ended and he went to work for his uncle, Alec Dixon, as a cowboy.

Hardin and some cousins—the Barekman brothers—herded cows all over the state for Dixon. They also drank, caroused, and gambled with fellow wranglers in every way fashionable at the time, including bets on how far you could spit, and mixed with men of questionable reputation like another sweet-natured buckaroo, soft drink sipper, and sometimes tearoom patron named Frank Polk.

Polk and John Wesley met and became bosom buddies and kindred spirits just long enough to gang up on and kill a poor soul named Tom Brady. Authorities caught and threw Polk in the calaboose for his efforts. He somehow managed a release in pretty short order. The inept Hardin accomplice then ended any chance for a historical reputation on par with his trail mate's when he got himself rudely shot to death a short time later while in the process of killing a Freestone County marshal named Charles Powers. Powers was evidently good enough with a gun to put some death dealing holes in Polk's quarrelsome hide, but not good enough to keep himself alive in the process.

Hardin again slipped through the clumsy fingers of military authorities and local law enforcement. He ran for the thickets and hoofed it north for the safer climes of the Red River country. Shortly after his arrival, he and another reputed cousin named Simp Dixon promptly got involved in a running gun battle with a squad of pursuing soldiers and killed two of them in the Richland Creek bottom.

Some historians question the veracity of this particular Hardin claim because no existing military records from the period make mention of it. Additionally the somewhat offhanded treatment of the fracas in his account of the incident could lead readers to feel he just might be blowing air up our skirts. Deep thinkers could wear out several cogs in the old gearbox trying to figure out why he would add bogus bodies to his count. Maybe the simplest one works best: In addition to being a cold-eyed killer, he was an unmitigated braggart who enjoyed his reputation and just couldn't resist the opportunity to appear even more dangerous to those who might challenge him later in life. Then again, it could have all been true.

Anyway, by December 25, 1869, a teenaged John Wesley had managed to kill at least five people (and maybe ten if you have a mind to believe everything the man claimed) when he and his brother Joe decided to attend the horse races at a well-known track near Towash out west of Hillsboro in Hill County. The brothers naturally indulged in all the popular pastimes of good, upright Christian southern boys back then. They drank everything in sight, bet the races, played cards, shot dice, and did anything else available that required laying down money on a chance to win more. A soiled dove would most likely have figured into the mix if they could've found one.

Hardin had a good day, ending up with more than $400 in his pocket, and capped it off late that night in a one-room log house playing cards with a pair of Arkansas hard cases named Ben Bradley and Hamp Davis. Bradley, Davis, and a Judge Moore evidently conspired to separate John Wesley from the pocket wad he probably would have later donated to a church. When they not only failed but also lost everything they had to the sixteen-year-old boy, the proverbial road apples hit the old wind-pushing device.

Bradley pulled a bowie knife the size of an Arab's scimitar and tried to slice the careless preacher's son. Seems John Wesley wanted to get comfortable during the evening's entertainment and had thrown his boots and pistol into the corner. A friend stepped between Hardin and the angry loser and gave the young rambling, gambling killer enough time to get outside still barefoot and unarmed.

Over the next hour or so, his friend James Collins tried to get John Wesley to cut his losses and head for home. But the angry, drunken boy wouldn't hear of it. The hard cases retired to a local dram shop about a hundred yards away from the log house and continued with a nonstop stream of vulgar-mouthed abuse shouted loud enough for good folks a mile away and asleep to hear.

Through a series of exchanges made by his friend Collins, John Wesley managed to get his hands on another pistol. As the two of them attempted to *peacefully* leave the scene and head for the safety of their individual homes, Bradley, at the head of an angry mob, attacked them. The Arkansas clod kicker fired first and missed. His second attempt snapped on a badly charged cylinder. By then the two men were damn near nose-to-nose, and

Hardin simply shot his opponent until he stopped pleading for mercy.

Although he does not mention it in his own version of the events, a Texas Ranger affidavit indicates there are those who believe Hardin also killed Judge Moore that same night. Either way the preacher's son had now dispatched at least six people for damn sure, maybe as many as twelve, and perhaps considerably more.

Hardin ran for home that night and consulted with his father—an action he took after almost every one of his deadly scrapes. They decided, again, that he probably should get away from the family home and visit for a spell with relatives.

Now here's where the often-bizarre tale of John Wesley Hardin's lethal career got really weird. About two weeks later he and his cousin Alec Barekman sought rest and refreshment in the little town of Horn Hill on their way to the hoped-for safety of his uncle Bob Hardin's home in Brenham. They tried to get a room in the only local five-star hotel but were turned away because the place was filled to the rafters with a troop of visiting circus performers. Clowns, jugglers, the bearded woman, animal trainers, fire-eaters, and magicians took up every horizontal surface in the rustic village. This unforeseen dose of fluky luck forced Hardin and his cousin to seek warmth and comfort with the remaining roustabout types who had campfires going on the edge of town.

Prior to John and Alec's arrival on the Horn Hill scene, some of the rougher element of the backwoods mud pie of a settlement indulged in shouting and shoving matches with members of the traveling circus' crew. Unaware of the tension, John Wesley made the mistake of bumping into one of the roustabouts as he tried to get closer to the fire.

In his own version of what happened next, Hardin naturally painted himself in the most flattering light possible by a seriously questionable assertion that he apologized profusely for his clumsy blunder and tried to make nice with the offended party. The brute he collided with threatened something along the lines of a broken proboscis for the boy's social *faux pas*. Hardin told him to bring it on, and the huge laborer smacked him in the nose so hard his eyes crossed. But on his way to the ground like a felled tree, our *pistolero joven* managed to maintain the presence of mind to pull his trusty blaster and shoot the circus worker betwixt his beady eyes. Barekman got a case of the twisted rope heebie-jeebies and decided to get away from his violent kinsman, who then continued on his way to Brenham once he'd regained consciousness and his eyes straightened out.

But before he could make it to his uncle's farm, he stopped in the town of Kosse for some much-needed rest and recreation after his tiring month-long rip of murder and chaos. The southwest Limestone County railroad town drew shady characters of all types, and John Wesley met a young woman of decidedly questionable virtue within minutes of his arrival. She invited him to her home that evening for a romantic *ren-dez-vousey*. Not long after they got comfortable for the evening, a man who claimed to be her husband broke down the bedroom door, waved a pistol around, and demanded payment of $100 to rectify this insult to his scarred honor.

As young as he was, Hardin evidently recognized the old badger game when he saw it even if he didn't know what to call it. He put on a big quaking act of mortal fear as he reached for his money and then dropped it at the thieving bastard's feet. When the badger bent over for the loot, John Wesley grabbed his own pistol and shot the man between the eyes. With the badger's surprised exit from this life, Hardin had, in the short span of three weeks, managed to kill at least seven people and possibly more. He scorched the earth and burned leaves off the trees getting from Kosse to the relative safety of his uncle's Brenham farm.

During his yearlong career as a tater digger and cow milker, the itinerant murderer continually rogued around the country for fifty miles in every direction. He claimed at that time to have met and become passing friends with gambler Phil Coe and famed Texas gunman Bill Longley. But for most of that time he laid low and restricted his activities to as little farm work as possible and an abbreviated bit of recreational gambling and drinking on the weekends. These activities—of which his aunt and uncle heartily disapproved—might well have brought him into contact with the likes of Coe and Longley.

As time passed, rumors of impending arrest put him on a meandering path of flight from Brenham to Round Rock and eventually Longview where state police impolitely threw him in jail for stealing a horse. When he managed to make bond on that charge, they snatched him up and threw him back in the pokey for stealing another pony and for the murder of a man named Hoffman in a Waco barbershop. Never one to dodge responsibility for a killing when given an opportunity to brag, Hardin nevertheless maintained that this particular charge was nothing more than a sack full of rancid East Texas meadow muffins.

While in custody, awaiting the move to Waco, he surreptitiously bought a loaded Colt .45 from one of his cellmates. He secreted the pistol with a loop of leather over his right shoulder and managed to keep his captors from finding it when they searched him before the almost 200 mile trip to McLennan County started.

On January 22, 1871, just a few miles outside of Waco, his senior escort, Lieutenant E.T. Stakes of the state police, left the boy in the care of Private Jim Smally while he proceeded to a nearby farmhouse to demand food for the men and their animals. Smally had not the slightest inkling of how dangerous his captive really was.

John Wesley waited until the two men had been alone for some minutes before he produced his hidden gun and shot Private Smally. In Hardin's rendition of the murder, our stalwart young gunman offers his opponent an opportunity to save himself by putting his hands in the air. Either Smally misheard the instructions, didn't fully understand what the hell was going on, or didn't have a snowball's chance in hell of saving himself anyway because he ended up dead as Julius Caesar in spite of Hardin's shouted instructions. Later most folks tended to agree that the bullet lodged in his chest was probably the shot that killed the poor doofus of a lawman.

As soon as he was sure Smally could no longer count himself amongst the living, John Wesley Hardin—killer of nine men in little more than two years—jumped on a horse and rode straight home to daddy's understanding open arms.

A Galveston newspaper's description of this particular shooting differed considerably from Hardin's version of the events. An aged black woman claimed to have witnessed the affair and testified that the murdered policeman had seated himself with his back to Hardin. She said that the killer pulled his pistol and fired while his opponent was preoccupied. Then Smally stood, turned, and tried to draw his own hand cannon at which time Hardin shot the man again in the stomach. The body was still on its way to the ground when John Wesley jumped on the lawman's horse and skedaddled. This second version just might be the more accurate one.

The Reverend Mr. Hardin must have been real close to reaching his last wit's end by that point. He recommended that his son head immediately for the safety of Mexico and not stop for anything until he crossed the border and had a tortilla in each hand. Our rambling, gambling teenage killer might have started in that direction, but he evidently had some kind of problem with his compass. He ended up about halfway between Belton and Waco where he happened upon three more policemen, who got the drop on him and took him into custody again.

Officers Smith, Jones, and Davis pointed our hero of the plains on his way to Austin and a sure-fire hanging, but they didn't get very far before they decided to stop for the night. While Hardin bided his time and kept his eyes open, the lawmen settled in for an evening of campfire stories, cowboy sing-alongs, toasted marshmallows, and real serious spider killer consumption. After a couple of hours of these nighttime fun and games, Davis and Jones collapsed drunkenly into their bedrolls and left the poor stupid Smith alone to guard a criminal whose homicidal tendencies were once again grossly underestimated.

By now any reader worth his salt should have picked up on a definite pattern in Hardin's bloodshed. As soon as the sentry's head hit his knees and he started to snore, John Wesley jumped up and grabbed the sleeping man's shotgun and officer Jones' pistol. He fired one barrel of the big blaster point blank into Smith's face and the second into Jones who still lay asleep on the ground. Davis sat up, realized what had occurred, and screamed, hollered, and begged for mercy. His seventeen-year-old executioner said, "I kept shooting him until I was satisfied he was dead."

The problem with this particular story is that we have only Hardin's word that it ever happened. But again, hey, why would he lie about it? The names are particularly commonplace and might have been used simply because he'd killed so many people by this point that he just couldn't remember them all. Or maybe he just made the whole thing up. This one is a classic example of one from column A or one from column B.

Anyway, if it happened, the fresh corpses still reeked and steamed when Hardin hotfooted it back to daddy with this newest tale of murder and insanity. This time James Hardin was evidently so upset that he not only told his son he "must" get himself south of the border, he even went so far as to escort the boy part of the way. You should have noticed that the operative phrase in that sentence was "part of the way."

As soon as the two men separated, the reverend's prodigal son headed for Gonzales where more family and friends resided and where he knew he'd be welcomed with open arms no matter how infamous his growing reputation. John Wesley's Aunt Martha had married Emanuel Clements Sr., and it was the safety of their home and the company of his eleven Clements cousins he sought in that famed Texas town.

The Clements brothers talked Wes into trailing cattle up the Chisholm Trail with them in an effort to stave off the very real prospects of a lynching the next time he got caught. In February 1871 he and his pack of cousins visited a Mexican camp on the cattle trail where the cards came out and the gambling started within minutes after they stepped down from their mounts.

During a game called Spanish monte that Hardin had never participated in and didn't understand, he demanded to be paid for a card that was actually a loser. The Mexican dealer tried to give the belligerent ignoramus some instructions on how the game was played and got a gun barrel across the noggin for his trouble.

Several of the staggered dealer's friends tried to come to his aid. One got a bullet in the arm, and the other was shot through the lungs. Prospects were pretty good that the lung shot was a deathblow, but no one in the Clements-Hardin crowd stuck around long enough to find out for sure. That didn't keep them from having a good laugh at the wounded Mexicans' expense later and for John Wesley to say that the best people in the vicinity at the time told him he had done a "good thing."

Emanuel Clements Sr. married Martha Balch Hardin, a sister of John Wesley Hardin's father. This huge clan thus became cousins to one of the West's most prolific killers. (Photo courtesy of Western History Collections, University of Oklahoma Libraries)

If you thought this out-of-control slaughterer of blacks, Mexicans, Yankee soldiers, and state policemen had even the slightest reserve of restraint, a single incident should put that idea to bed real fast. An aggressive, troublesome white steer that drifted into the herd Hardin had charge of caused him so many headaches that he shot the animal in the eye. The poor beast, having no weapon with which to defend itself, immediately and unceremoniously died. Needless to say the poor creature's owner found out about the episode and was sorely put upon as a result of the loss. Seems the animal was a family pet raised from a calf by his blind four-year-old daughter. Okay, maybe not! Whatever the steer's real or imagined history, John Wesley later lamented that the creature's owner caused him a world of trouble in the courts and that he ended up spending over $200 dollars to straighten out that angry steer-killing episode.

A few days after he murdered the poor innocent albino bovine, his trail herd crossed into the Indian Nations. On the South Canadian River, he diligently searched for and finally spotted a real live Native American heathen hiding in a bush and claimed the savage fired an arrow at him—bad mistake on the poor red man's part. Wes shot him d.r.t. (dead right there).

Shortly after that killing, which he later admitted he looked forward to committing, he got into it with some Osage folks over a stolen bridle. The Osage gentleman Hardin believed responsible for the theft made the mistake of also trying to cut a cow from the Clements herd. The two men argued. The Osage man killed the steer, and John Wesley shot the hell out of the Indian gentleman. If you've bothered to keep count, the dead now numbered at least fifteen and perhaps considerably more that he just didn't bother to mention in his own personal gory memoir.

In spite of all the blood he'd already spilled—just in his short career as a cowboy—the number of dead Mexicans and Indians was about to take a quantum leap into the realm of lethal lunacy. Once all the Clements-Hardin dogies forded the Little Arkansas River and made it to an area near modern day Valley Center, Kansas, a Mexican herd caught up with them and some of their steers got mixed in with the bunch Wes controlled.

Naturally an argument broke out. Hell, if Hardin had anything to do with it, what could you expect by now? Shouting and swearing turned into exchanged gunfire. The vaqueros made the mistake of backing off long enough for Hardin and Jim Clements to get themselves armed with the best weapons in camp. When the smoke finally cleared, after the ensuing horseback pistol fight, the Texas cousins agreed that the barely eighteen-year-old boy had managed to personally dispatch five of the six pesky Mexicans eradicated in the fracas. By his own numbers John Wesley Hardin now admitted to having ended the lives of some twenty people between the 1868 death of Mage Holshousen and the boatload of Mexicans he murdered on the trail to Abilene in 1871.

Cowboys—Mexican or otherwise—should have hit their knees and thanked God almighty when the fiery Texan finally reached Kansas' most famous cow town and the *somewhat* restraining presence of a city marshal named Wild Bill Hickok. But even a man of Hickok's commanding presence and ready fame couldn't avoid being dragged into the mud and the blood and madness of Wes Hardin's cyclonic life. A confrontation with the deadliest lawman and pistol fighter in the Old West became one of the most enduring legends in Hardin's career of murder and havoc.

By the time John Wesley arrived in Abilene, James Butler Hickok had been the chief marshal of the city's police force for about six months. Shortly after the six-foot tall, thirty-four-year-old, already famed pistoleer received his appointment to Abilene's head law enforcement position, well-known Texas gamblers and gunmen Ben Thompson and Phil Coe arrived in town. They opened a home for wayward cowboys named the Bull's Head Saloon. Friction between Hickok and the gamblers was immediate and raucous. The Texans claimed the new marshal persecuted them for no good reason, and Hickok countered their accusations by telling everyone within earshot that the sleazy gamblers cheated the drovers anytime they got a chance.

But even Wild Bill's charges of cheating didn't compare to what really set those ol' Texas boys' teeth on edge. No, the thing that got their goat, so to speak, involved the new marshal's abuse of the sign they put up over the entrance to the Bull's Head. Seems the illustration vividly portrayed a huge long-horned animal gifted with massive and obvious masculine equipment. Respectable people—defined as women who weren't whores—found the portrait offensive, objected to its prominent display of heavy-duty calf making possibilities, and complained bitterly to the marshal. Hickok, who knew righteous indignation when he saw it, sent a crew of carpenters to deal with the sign when the Texans refused to take it down. They smeared a thick layer of paint over the distasteful aspects of its male anatomy.

Thompson and Coe had an immediate collective fit and from that day forward looked for any opportunity to make Wild Bill's life as difficult as possible without endangering themselves in the process. Enter hotheaded John Wesley Hardin, young, reckless, and already well known to every cowboy in Abilene as a dangerous man killer who just might be influenced to do something about their problem.

Fellow Texan Ben Thompson, a well-known gambler, gunfighter, and occasional lawman, co-owned the Bull's Head Saloon on First Street in Abilene with another noted Lone Star gunman, Phil Coe. They butted heads with Wild Bill over a celebrated sign that featured a virile bull and tried to get Hardin to kill the famed shootist. (Photo courtesy of Western History Collections, University of Oklahoma Libraries)

Ben Thompson bitterly complained to Hardin about Hickok's damned Yankee sensibilities. He more than implied that the blue-bellied, law-enforcing bully tended to pick Southern men out for the undertaker's attention anytime he wanted to add another notch to the grips of his .36-caliber Navy Colts. Hardin was intelligent enough to recognize Thompson's game and informed the angry gambler that if Hickok needed killing he'd have to do it himself. Even a man of Wes' reputation understood that no matter how skilled or lucky you might be, a gunfighter of Hickok's well-documented ability could easily put you in a cold, dark grave.

This didn't keep Hardin from boldly and openly carrying two pistols on his person everywhere he went in spite of signs posted all over town that forbade such conduct. Crowds trailed around town after him in the hope that they would be present when Hickok jerked the boy up by his roots. But no one witnessed the incident that supposedly brought the whole thing to a head.

As Hardin told the story, Hickok confronted him one day while he was in the midst of consuming vast quantities of adult beverages and rolling a game of ten pins. (For those of you in the *far west* Big Bend area of Texas, that was an early form of bowling.) The marshal pulled one of his ivory handled revolvers and told the boy to give up his weapons. Hardin said he wouldn't do it and then followed an angry Hickok into the street. Pistol still firmly in hand, the famed lawman turned, faced John Wesley, and demanded once again that he surrender his firearms. At that point Hardin said he would, pulled his side arms, and held them out to Hickok, butts first. As the lawman reached for them, Wes did his rendition of the famed border roll, a move that quickly reverses the position of the pistols and ends with them pointed and cocked at your adversary. The most famous lawman in the West at that time was so impressed he did a

Wild Bill Hickok pictured at the height of his prowess as the West's most dangerous pistoleer and much the way he would probably have appeared during John Wesley Hardin's bloody 1871 visit to Abilene, Kansas. (Photo courtesy of Western History Collections, University of Oklahoma Libraries)

quick-talking tap-dance designed to save his own life and managed to get Wes back in the bar where they retired to a private room and got drunk together like life-long trail buddies. Later that evening they supposedly parted good friends. At least that's what Hardin claimed.

As previously mentioned, a small problem exists with this particular load of Hardin horse fritters. No one who accompanied him on the Abilene trip managed to retain any living memory of the confrontation. Hickok never mentioned it. No newspaper descriptions exist of it. Gip Clements wrote that he never heard cousin Wes talk of any such event. He did say that Hardin had "faced Bill down," but he never explained where or when it happened.

Probably the most powerful argument against Hardin's version of the story rests in the simple fact that Wild Bill Hickok—a deadly pistoleer and a man not widely known as an idiot—for unfathomable reasons didn't kill a dangerous and unpredictable lunatic when standing in the street with a cocked pistol pointed squarely at the problem's heart. Even more telling, you'd think that a man of Hickok's vast experience in the realm of gunplay would have immediately recognized Hardin's border roll ruse to begin with.

Well, a drunken Hardin went directly from the highly questionable Hickok confrontation to a restaurant with a friend and immediately got into an argument with a bunch of rowdies who loudly started pickin' on Texans. Hardin took issue with the obnoxious dirt balls, threw down on the whole insufferable bunch, challenged everyone there to put his manhood on display, and went to blasting.

The big talking little doers all scattered, but one poor slub couldn't run fast enough, and John Wesley shot him in the head just as the terrified man made it to the door. The body dropped into a bloody pile of teeth that had scattered all over the boardwalk when the bullet exited through the man's mouth. Hardin stepped over the oozing corpse, backed everyone away from the door, mounted his horse, and kicked it for the Clements cattle bedding grounds on the Cottonwood River about thirty-five miles away.

He'd only been hiding out on the Cottonwood for a short time when several well-known cattlemen came to him with a request that he apprehend a Mexican killer named Bideno. The evil, gutless vaquero had murdered a popular cowboy named Billy Cohron. Cohron, trail boss for O.W. Wheeler, and Señor Bideno argued over some orders the Mexican didn't particularly care for, and when the smoke cleared Cohron had somehow managed to get himself shot in the back. Hardin agreed that the homicide was "foul and treacherous." If the cattle owners needed an expert on "foul and treacherous" they had surely found one.

Before he accepted the job though, Wes insisted on being provided a warrant for Bideno's arrest, appointment as a deputy sheriff, and letters of introduction to trail bosses he might meet during his search who could help him out.

As a full-fledged lawdog-type deputy sheriff and commissioned bounty hunter, Wes primed his pistols and headed south in the company of a cowboy named Jim Rogers. They hoped to catch Bideno before he reached the Indian Nations and if not then, for sure before he got back to the great Lone Star State. By the sheerest of chances they ran into a South Texas herd coming up the Chisholm Trail. Billy Cohron's brother John and a close family friend named Hugh Anderson were working the drive. They decided to quit and assist Sheriff Hardin and Rogers in the chase.

The "posse" found Bideno in Sumner City, Kansas. They had split into two groups at the time. John Wesley and Hugh Anderson encountered the Mexican killer first in a combination restaurant-saloon. Our friendly neighborhood doer of good deeds, deputy sheriff, and sometime destroyer of men claimed the high road again in his version of the events that followed their discovery. Seems Bideno had ordered lunch, just said grace, and was about to eat when Hardin and Anderson confronted him with pistols drawn.

John Wesley claimed that he told his prey no harm would come to him so long as he gave up and did as he was told. The wily vaquero evidently didn't believe him. He went a reachin' and a grabbin' and ended up with a bullet in the skull before his fingers could wrap themselves around the grips of his weapons.

Billy Cohron's brother and Jim Rogers rushed in from the street when they heard the shooting. Cohron wanted to put some more holes in the obviously dead Bideno just for the fun of it, but our noble hero and protector of Mexican corpses prevented it. At least he said he did.

A crowd of Sumner City's finest citizens quickly gathered outside the saloon, and Hardin found it necessary to explain his actions to the locals in a blistering oration that resulted in commendations all around for him and his party of noble searchers and shooters.

That town had no newspaper, but the nearby settlement of Oxford did and it ran a story about Bideno's meld with the eternal that differed considerably from the Hardin version of events. According to the *Oxford Times*, a man named Conway (perhaps a confused version of Cohron—newspaper reporters were known to drink a bit back then) took the law into his own hands and killed an unnamed man he claimed was Mexican in an act of revenge for the murder of his brother. The *Times* reporter went so far as to describe the Mexican as "unconscious" of the certain death that approached him as he had lunch. Seems the unaware, unarmed, and supposed Mexican died after being shot in the head while sipping coffee and ended up sitting in the chair with the steaming cup still pressed to his dead lips.

Whatever did or didn't happen and whoever was or wasn't there, John Wesley ended up back in Abilene where he claimed that grateful citizens pressed considerable money into his palms for a job well done. But the whole affair from his back-shooting murder of the loudmouth in Abilene till his return from Sumner City makes little if any real sense to a discerning examiner of the available facts.

Abilene law enforcement's lack of action in the "from behind" skull shot just before he became a deputy begs considerable questioning. Then, on top of that, you have to ask yourself why on earth would anyone in his right mind make John Wesley Hardin—an infamous *Texas* man killer—a *Kansas* deputy sheriff and give him an arrest warrant for anyone? And who in the hell deputized him in the first place? That is if anyone ever really did. Oh the questions that can abound if you set your mind free.

Anyway, Hardin took a much-needed break to rest the blister on his trigger finger and for about a month somehow managed not to put any new corpses in the ground. Troops of angels must have celebrated that period of quiet from the first week in July 1871 till August 6. Then what could arguably be the most famous (or infamous, depending on your viewpoint) John Wesley Hardin killing of them all took place in Abilene's American Hotel.

That fateful night a drunken Gip Clements and his cousin John Wesley stumbled to their room after partying at one church social after another, fell into their flea-bitten beds, and tried to go to sleep. In the stall next door a doomed goober named Charles Cougar had already made it to dreamland and snored so loud the rickety board wall separating the men rattled like a tin roof in a windstorm.

Chapter 3

After yelling several times for the noisy neighbor to roll the hell over, Hardin's temper finally got the best of him. He grabbed his smoke pole and fired at least four shots through the single plank wall. The snoring stopped immediately and after duly noting that he just might have fired a bit low, Hardin and his cousin realized that poor Mr. Cougar would not be waking up. At least that's the legend. A highly questionable legend told, retold, and told again for almost a hundred and fifty years. Repeated so often that most people to this very day (many of whom should know better) tell the tale as though it is cold, hard fact.

John Wesley's version of the events as noted in his autobiography differed somewhat. In fact they were nothing close to the legend. He claimed that as he drifted off to sleep, an armed thief entered his room and stole his pants. As the scurvy bandit made for the door, Hardin fired four shots at the man who stumbled into the hallway, fell into a massive pool of his own blood, and promptly gave up the ghost.

Newspapers of the era reported several different versions of the murder. One said Cougar was seated on his bed reading the newspaper when someone promiscuously fired several shots through the wall, one of which hit him in the heart and killed him instantly. Another of the local rags reported that two disgruntled former business partners of Cougar's entered his room, assassinated him, escaped, and were never apprehended.

The reader now has four versions of the same story from a variety of different sources. Pick the one you like most and it should be as good as any of the others. Or perhaps you're a traditionalist and believe anything other than the killing of a man simply for snoring is just another windy whizzer not worth a second's consideration.

It didn't matter anyway, because John Wesley had finally and irrevocably worn out his bloody welcome in Abilene, Kansas.

Several posses beat the bushes and brambles of the surrounding countryside for him and his luckless cousin. Hardin later wrote that Hickok would surely have killed him given an opportunity, and the threat must have been enough to convince him to hightail it back to Texas and family.

He hadn't been in Gonzales more than a heartbeat when he discovered things had heated up some during his absence and the Texas State Police wanted a large chunk of his murderous behind more than ever.

On October 6, 1871, a black state police officer named Green Paramore got the drop on Hardin in a Nopal, Texas grocery store. The panicky lawman demanded his captive's pistols, and John Wesley offered them to him butts first. As Paramore gingerly reached for the big Colts, they spun in the hands of his prisoner and spewed several rounds of hot lead into the surprised policeman's head. Outside, a second officer, John Lackey, who guarded the entrance of the store from the back of his mule, realized what had happened and started blasting away at Hardin. Wes returned fire and his was more accurate. Though wounded in the mouth, Lackey managed to escape by riding his mule into a lake and stayed alive by floating with nothing but his nose above water.

Black citizens of Gonzales County were madder'n hell about the shootings and threatened to go on a rampage and burn out or kill all the whites. Governor Edmund Davis tried to head off what was cooking up to be a wide-open race war. On November fifth he posted a reward of $400 for the arrest of someone named Wesley Clements alias Wesley Hardin. A posse of black policemen with dollar signs in their eyes hotfooted it to Gonzales from Austin. Wes got wind of the pack of lawmen, armed himself to the teeth, met them in the woods, and killed three of his stunned enemies. The rest hightailed it back to the capital.

Chapter 3

This photograph is believed to be a wedding portrait taken of John Wesley Hardin to commemorate his February 29, 1872 marriage to fourteen-year-old Jane Bowen. (Photo courtesy of Western History Collections, University of Oklahoma Libraries)

As our hero said, they returned home a group of "sadder but wiser men."

In February 1872 he married a fourteen-year-old girl named Jane Bowen, and although his devotion to her seemed genuine, Hardin continued to play the part of rambling, gambling, murderous rogue. He rarely spent more than a few weeks at a time with his new bride, but it was enough to produce a child by Jane's fifteenth birthday.

Hardin revealed little about his child bride in his memoirs. A photograph of her—said to have been taken the day of their wedding—depicts a slightly built but fiercely determined looking young woman whose haunted countenance probably reveals more about the uncertainty of life during that period of history than any minute by minute retelling of John Wesley Hardin's violent and sadistic existence ever could.

In May 1872 Wes left Jane, hit the trail again, and rogued all over South Texas until early August. During that period he may or may not have killed several more Mexicans. At any rate, he stopped in Trinity City for a bit of drinking, gambling, and ten pins with a violence-prone farmer named George Sublett. Sublett also sported a bloody reputation for murdering blacks after the Civil War ended.

Hardin's deadly pattern played itself out to the very letter. The men got into a face-slapping argument over the results of their ten pins game, and Sublett stomped out of the saloon in search of a weapon. Hardin went behind the bar to retrieve his own pistols just in time to be confronted outside the door by his raging opponent, who cut loose with both barrels of a shotgun. The blast peppered Wes with several large buckshot pellets, two of which entered near the gunfighter's navel and flattened out next to his backbone and ribs.

A badly wounded Wes Hardin pursued the first assailant to draw his blood down the street and managed to shoot Sublett in the shoulder before his own painful injuries forced him to give up the chase. A doctor named Carrington—using a knife, forceps, and no painkillers—operated on the wounded killer and dug the pellets out. Wes must have considered himself damned lucky that the slugs didn't do any serious internal damage—other than punch a hole in one of his kidneys—or that infection didn't set in. If either had occurred, his career as a serial murderer would have ended right then and there.

Indictments were issued, posses hit the trail, and Wes fled to Sumpter where he laid low and tried to recover. But a determined search forced him to flee from one friendly household to the next until the state police caught him at the home of his friend Dave Harrel. During the blistering gunfight that followed, he killed another lawman and ended up getting shot in the leg for his efforts. He had by that point snuffed the candles of something in the neighborhood of thirty men, but now he also suffered from a debilitating stomach wound and a new hole in his upper thigh.

Confronted with the possibility of a lingering death from his wounds, Hardin gave himself up to Sheriff Dick Regan, who saw that the injured outlaw got proper medical treatment before transferring him to Austin and the questionable care of Travis County officials.

He stayed in a dungeon-like Austin jail until being transferred back to Gonzales where an old friend, Sheriff Bill Jones, helped him escape on November 19, 1872. Jones later said that the six sentries who were supposed to be guarding Hardin must have all gone to sleep on duty at the same time. In an effort to save a little bit of face with state officials, Jones offered a $100 reward for the capture and return of Texas's most infamous killer. Why not? Hell, he knew no one would try to collect it.

In 1873 John Wesley Hardin, alias Wes Clements, alias Little Arkansas, alias Young Seven-up, got himself involved in one of the longest and deadliest feuds in the history of Texas. The Sutton-Taylor blood bath's origins, length, and complexity were such that a detailed examination will not be attempted in these pages. (If you're really interested consult C.L. Sonnichsen's classic story of Texas's great feuds *I'll Die Before I'll Run* for the absolute definitive account.) Suffice it to say that Hardin fell in with the anti-Reconstruction, former Confederate Taylor clan. They took great pleasure in rubbing out as many pro-Reconstruction, blue-bellied Yankee, Texas State Police supporting bastards in the Sutton bunch as they could find. Hardin's hatred for the Sutton clan ran deep and wide.

On or about the first week of August in 1873, Jim Taylor and Wes caught the universally despised Jack Helm—a former Texas State Police officer, Sutton camp leader, and partisan—in Albuquerque, Texas, and shotgunned the hell out of him. Helm, too far from his own arsenal and armed with only a knife, never had so much as a steer's chance in a meat packing plant of defending himself. Stories exist that Jim Taylor emptied a Colt .45 into Helm's head after Hardin brought him down with a shotgun. Seems Taylor just wanted to make damned sure Helm didn't get up again, so he turned the man's brain box into a flour sifter.

Over the next year or so John Wesley managed not to kill anyone of any particular note. He did get involved in several shooting scrapes as a result of his association with the Taylor bunch. A number of peace treaties between the two warring factions were signed, but they turned out to be worth even less than any of those made with the original inhabitants of the West. Then in May 1874 he finally committed the murder that would eventually put an end to the John Wesley Hardin everyone had come to know and love so much.

In order to keep a good face on his gambling, Hardin and his brother Joe bought and sold cattle—or at least they said they did. Whether those rough-as-a-cob dogies just could have been stolen or appropriated in a less than legal manner seemed not to bother the Hardin boys in the least. And besides, once you got a cow more than two or three counties away from its point of origin, the folks who might want to buy it from you could have cared less whose brand it carried anyway. On top of all that, Joe Hardin was a skilled lawyer and *always* had a bill of sale for his cows whether he bought them or not.

Anyway, John Wesley started north from Cuero with a herd destined for Wichita. This trip had more than a little bit to do with the fact that he again needed to get out of Texas for a while. His cousin Joe Clements acted as trail boss for the venture, and they stopped in Comanche to pick up a sizable number of other cows that lawyer Hardin had acquired by what can only be described as highly complex and questionable means.

Chapter 3

Most of the questions came from a party of irate cattlemen from Brown County, who had no use for the Hardin brothers. They pressured county sheriff J.H. Gideon to do something about what they referred to as the *Hardin Gang*. He told his deputy, a well-liked and much respected former Texas Ranger named Charles Webb, to look into the matter.

One of the first things Webb did was to go out and arrest Jim Waldrip and James Beard, a couple of Hardin family friends widely reputed to be cattle thieves. He threw them in the Brown County jail, but feelings ran so hot from locals that a lynching seemed imminent. In an effort to prevent violence, he moved both men to the Williamson County lockup in Georgetown. John Wesley heard about this atrocity the third week in May while visiting with Waldrip's mother and agreed that deputy Webb was a lowlife scum-sucking son of a bitch and should be put in his place.

On May 26, 1874, Hardin visited Comanche to celebrate his twenty-first birthday. Folks from miles around attended a yearly festival going on at the time, and a carnival was cranked up full tilt on the edge of town. All the local beer joints, honky-tonks, cantinas, and cow country watering holes were going full blast. Local drunks and sporting men of every stripe came out of the woodwork. John Wesley spent the morning at the racetrack and managed to win a huge pile of money, wagons, and other people's animals with his stud, Rondo.

After he'd put damn near every man in Comanche County afoot, he headed for town and spent the afternoon strolling from one saloon to the next where he threw money around like it was confetti and soaked up enough whiskey to float the paddle wheeler *Yellowstone*.

His little brother Jeff tried to get him away from the drunkenness and dissolution for a family celebration of his birthday. But on the way out of town Wes made the boy stop their buggy when they passed the liquor locker of Jack Wright located on the northeast corner of the Comanche town square.

Young Jeff watched as his older brother oozed out of the wagon and wobbled inside to continue his drunken celebration. Comanche Sheriff John Carnes through his deputy Frank Wilson tried to get Wes to go home. Wilson escorted the intoxicated gunfighter outside and about ten steps away from the front door onto a back street near the saloon. They stood there and argued about whether Hardin needed to leave or not, just as Deputy Sheriff Charles Webb walked up.

Hardin said friends had warned him that Webb and a posse of men from Brown County had arrived in town to kill him and his friend Jim Taylor. He stopped and challenged Webb by aggressively asking if the deputy had an arrest warrant for either man. Webb replied that he didn't even know who Hardin was. When John Wesley enlightened the lawman as to his identity, Webb said no he didn't have any outstanding papers for the mouthy murderer's arrest.

At that point a seemingly gregarious Hardin invited the deputy inside for a drink and a good cigar. Webb accepted, but as Wes turned away, Sheriff Carnes' brother Dave or a friend named Bud Dixon yelled, "Look out, Jack!" Hardin claimed that Webb was in the process of drawing one of his two guns (or maybe scratching his nose) and that he pulled his own pistol as they fired at about the same time. Webb's shot put a nasty glancing wound in Hardin's side, but John Wesley's slug hit Webb in the cheek. He was probably already dead when Jim Taylor and Bud Dixon shot the bejabbers out of him on his way to a blood soaked mud hole on the ground.

It was the single biggest mistake our serial murderin' South Texas preacher's son ever made. He didn't know it at the time, but his life was essentially over in spite of the fact that it would take another twenty-one years for death to finally come for him.

Hardin and his cronies immediately found out in no uncertain terms just how popular Charlie Webb really was. An angry, vocal, and aggressive crowd quickly gathered around the dead lawman and forced Wes and his friends to retreat behind drawn pistols. He, Jim Taylor, Alec Barekman, and Ham Anderson headed for the bushes and the hoped-for safety that distance from his crimes had always provided in the past.

Rangers put the entire Hardin clan under house arrest. When Joe got back to town the next day on May 27 after bringing his brother fresh horses and supplies, he and friends Tom and Bud Dixon were locked up in a two-story stone house on the town square supposedly in order to keep them from acting as spies.

Wes' traveling companions, Barekman and Anderson, quickly tired of sleeping on the ground and being chased all over the country. They left Hardin and holed up in the home of a farmer named William Stone near Bucksnort Creek. Sheriff Carnes and a passel of Texas Rangers cornered them on the afternoon of June 1 and killed the hell out of the two Hardin cronies in the gun battle that followed.

That night a party of heavily armed outstanding and upright citizens from Brownwood broke into the stone house where Joe Hardin was being detained. They disarmed the guards and dragged Joe and the Dixon brothers out for a little cow pasture necktie party and marshmallow roasting. The terrified lawyer vigorously protested the proceedings, but it just didn't matter. The vigilantes strung all three of them up while a sizable crowd of Comanche's citizens watched.

Perhaps for the first time in his blood-spattered life John Wesley got the message. He fled to Florida with his wife and children where he assumed the name John Swain and bought a saloon in Gainesville from a man named Samuel Burnett.

He hadn't been in town long when the local sheriff got into a fight in front of his saloon and deputized owner Swain on the spot for some much-needed assistance. The law-abiding Mr. Swain unceremoniously went to work and pistol whipped one man and shot another. Shortly after that incident the jail mysteriously burned to the ground at the hands of a party of masked men said to have been led by John Swain. The hoosegow was occupied at the time by a black man named Eli, accused of having raped a white woman.

Pressure from detectives on his trail forced him to move several times after the Gainesville shooting, and the Texas reward of $4,000 for delivery of his body back to Travis County really caused things to heat up. Finally, on August 23, 1877, after almost three years, Ranger John Armstrong led a combined party of Texas and Florida lawmen who captured Hardin in Pensacola, Florida, after a brutal fist and gunfight on a train headed back to his home near Pollard, Alabama.

Some serious finagling with the laws of several states was required in order to keep Hardin on the rails to Texas, but Armstrong and his cohort Jack Duncan did manage to get him back to Austin. In September Wes was escorted to Comanche for a trial that took only two days, and on the twenty-eighth of that month a jury sentenced him to twenty-five years in the Texas State Penitentiary for the *second-degree murder* of Charlie Webb. His appeal took a year but was denied when the sentencing judge didn't buy his failed argument of self-defense.

On October 5, 1878, the twenty-five-year-old man, who could arguably have been the most prolific murderer the mythic West ever saw, entered the Texas state prison system as Convict #7109. After a number of attempted escapes ended in serious, body-rending floggings at the hands of experienced guards, he evidently had a revelation and discovered that Jesus was sleeping in the bunk next to his. Five years of willful, angry,

Captain John Armstrong led the party of lawmen who captured Hardin in Pensacola, Florida, on August 23, 1877. (Photo courtesy of Western History Collections, University of Oklahoma Libraries)

and violent behavior disappeared. He became a model prisoner, hymn singing Sunday school teacher, and student of the law. On February 17, 1894, he walked out of the penitentiary a free but seriously changed man. By that point his wife had passed away, his children couldn't have picked him out of a lineup, and the end of his life was little more than a year down a dusty trail that led to El Paso.

Upon his release back into society, John Wesley soon discovered that going straight is always easier when you're behind bars and temptation can't get at you. By a convoluted and circuitous route that included a second marriage to a fifteen-year-old girl that failed within weeks, he ended up in Texas's most famous border town where death had patiently awaited his alcohol-soaked arrival. Its name was John Selman.

Hardin put out a shingle shortly after he arrived in El Paso where he defended his distant cousin Killin' Jim Miller on a charge of conspiring to rid the ground of Reeves County sheriff Bud Frazer's shadow. After the trial ended with an acquittal, Miller made good on his past efforts when he caught Frazer at a poker table in Toya, Texas, and put so many buckshot holes in the man you could've read the *El Paso Times* through his perforated hide. Other than that single case, John Wesley did very little lawyerin' and a whole lot of liquor-lubricated bragging about the past.

On or about April 7, 1895, a woman named Beulah Morose (see *Texas Bad Girls: Hussies, Harlots, and Horse Thieves* for a more detailed rendition of this part of the Hardin story) retained him to represent the interests of her husband, Martin, who was locked up in a Juarez, Mexico, jail awaiting extradition on a charge of cattle theft. During the course of their relationship she moved in with Hardin, and by the time Mexican authorities released her husband, poor ole Martin was baffled, bewildered, broke, and stuck in Mexico.

Morose's friends tried to reason with the drunken former pistoleer but didn't make much headway, and after some careful consideration, Hardin must have decided that the best course of action was to jerk the former New Mexico cattle thief up by his roots at the first available opportunity. But he evidently didn't want to do the killing himself. There's the very real probability that he recognized the possibility of a quick return to prison and just didn't want to take a chance. Evidence exists that he might have made some kind

John Selman Sr. sat for this photo in 1878 some seventeen years before he killed Wes Hardin on August 19, 1895. Hardin played dice at the time and had his back to Selman. The old marshal claimed that scurvy dog went for his gun. Self-defense, don't you know. (Photo courtesy of Western History Collections, University of Oklahoma Libraries)

of a deal with Constable John Selman, Deputy Marshal George Scarborough, and several other well- known local lawmen. They all plotted to snuff Morose's candle and share in any monetary proceeds left over afterward, including a nice-sized New Mexico reward for the fugitive cattle thief's head.

On the night of June 29, 1895, Martin Morose slipped across the border from Juarez by way of the Mexican Central Railroad Bridge. He was under the mistaken impression—given to him by George Scarborough—his panting wife, Beulah, waited for a frisky reconciliation in the sunflower patch on the Texas side of the river.

Surprise! Surprise! Just as he and his friend Scarborough's feet hit Texas soil, Deputy Marshal Jeff Milton, Texas Ranger Frank McMahan, and perhaps Constable John Selman opened fire. In this instance Morose *wasn't* dead when he hit the ground. Stories say that Scarborough stood on the man's chest and that someone shot the wounded cattle thief through the heart at least two more times —just to make sure you know.

Whatever did or didn't take place that night and whoever was or wasn't involved, Scarborough, Jeff Milton, and Frank McMahan were all charged with murder in the affair, but they were eventually acquitted for lack of evidence. More importantly some kind of falling out about the monetary split took place between the conspirators, and on

Jeff Milton served as Deputy U.S. Marshal at the time of Hardin's death. He, George Scarborough, and Frank McMahan are believed to have conspired with Hardin and others to kill cattle thief Martin Morose. They were placed on trial for the crime, but, typical of the time, everyone got acquitted for lack of evidence. (Photo courtesy of Western History Collections, University of Oklahoma Libraries)

August 19, 1895, at around 11 p.m. Selman caught Hardin with his back turned while shooting dice in the Acme Saloon and rendered him deader'n Andy-By-God-Jackson with a bullet to the back of the head that passed through a sizable portion of his brain and came out over his left eye. There is plenty of existing proof that Hardin's alcohol consumption at the time was such that he never knew what hit him. You'd have to admit it was a sad but somewhat fitting end to the most feared pistol fighter who ever walked the dusty streets of Texas myth and reality.

One of the first American motion pictures ever produced was a western. The general public's concept of heroes and villains from the period of our national history portrayed therein is derived almost totally from the visual images generated by the films and television shows that followed *The Great Train Robbery* for the next eighty years.

But the psychological and social complexity of those men and women who actually lived the lives portrayed in movies and television shows about the American West has never achieved the level of reality some of us would like to see. Unfortunately myth and legend have always sold better than authenticity. The life of a man like John Wesley Hardin could serve as a good example of this thesis.

Hardin's defenders usually portray him in a relatively positive light. Many still consider him little more than a good-looking, well-mannered gentleman who only killed those who *needed* it and feel that he never shot anyone except in the act of preserving his own life. Even if that were true and he had just managed to rub out thirty or twenty or ten instead of the probable fifty he claimed, there would have to be a certain

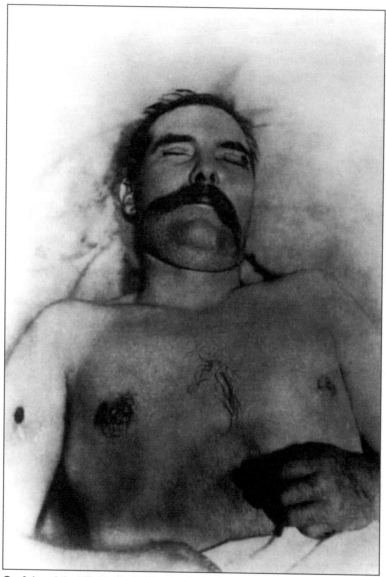

Gunfighter John Wesley Hardin shortly after his death on August 19, 1895. The wound at the corner of his left eye is where John Selman's bullet to the head made its exit. (Photo courtesy of Western History Collections, University of Oklahoma Libraries)

number of those unfortunate dead who did not fit the self-preservation defense of his bloody actions.

The truth seems to be that John Wesley Hardin started killing people at an astonishingly early age, and he continued to rid
the planet of human beings at an appalling rate until he murdered the wrong man and ended up in prison for it.

If such a criminal existed today he would quickly find himself on the FBI's top ten most wanted serial killer list faster
than a roadrunner can jump on a June bug. True, we do live in a
different time and place, but Hardin's sins against humanity bor-
dered on a one-man plague of biblical proportions, and his
murderous life has never been adequately portrayed for the
huge audience out there that still has little idea of who he was
and how he lived and died. But his place in the pantheon of
Texas killers was assured less than a year after he murdered
Mage Holshousen.

This Colt single action Army .45-caliber revolver, serial number 126680, was one
of two pistols found on the body of John Wesley Hardin. (Photo courtesy of
Western History Collections, University of Oklahoma Libraries)

Chapter 4

The Deacon of Death

Killin' Jim Miller

There is a saying used in the business world to describe how simple the corporation's newest Byzantine decision, product announcement, or procedural guideline is to understand. It goes something like this, "You don't have to be a rocket scientist to understand Yabba-Dabba-Doo." However, a problem exists with that all-purpose aphorism. Sometimes in this life you not only need to have an advanced degree in guided missile propellants to comprehend what in the blue-eyed hell's going on, you might even need to have had a personal relationship with Werner Von Braun to begin to grasp how goofy things can get when it comes to people and how they think.

Such is the case with murderers, thieves, gamblers, and reprobates of all types and descriptions from our historic past. No matter how profoundly depraved they might have been, there's usually someone who will come to their aid and comfort with reassuring words of goodwill and try to explain away inexplicable behavior and paint a good face on their appalling actions.

It might be difficult for some people to believe, but a theory exists that in the Old West there lived "good" and "bad" killers. Perhaps the more specific difference would best be described as those considered "wicked" and the others thought of as "respectable." Amazing isn't it that such a thing could even be imagined or considered.

According to this hypothesis, the wicked man killed for personal gain by way of accumulating filthy lucre once he had blasted holes in his target's hide. The respectable killer pulled his man's picket pin in order to preserve his family's good name or to keep the other fellow from driving him in the ground like a tent peg.

Use of this odd set of guidelines renders John Wesley Hardin, who by his own count murdered approximately fifty people, "respectable" or "good" in the overall philosophy of how killers did their bloody business. This in spite of the fact that at least some of his slayings obviously weren't done to preserve his family's honor or save his murderous hide. All too often he kept bad company, drank a tub-full of less than quality liquor, picked a fight, and then shot someone dead for little or no reason. True, he did dispatch more than a few for trying to fit him with a pitchfork for the Great Beyond. But if you look at many of those sorry episodes very closely, they also seemed to follow a pattern of drunkenness, belligerent encounters, gunfire, and the death of anyone other than John Wesley.

Killin' Jim Miller was a whole different story. He would have to be considered a "wicked" murderer because he possessed no discernable sense of honor, not one measly scruple in his entire body, and did most of his gory work from behind his opponents, covered with the safety of darkness and in the manner of what most people would consider as cowardly. The oddest thing about this theoretical bag of bull feathers is that these two vastly different—but very similar—men eventually became distant relatives by way of marriage.

We don't know as much about Killin' Jim as John Wesley because Miller didn't leave behind a detailed autobiography as did his distant cousin. He normally conducted his life of foul murder from the misty blue-black of darkness and a nicely established line of thick trees. Only a few of his killings were witnessed by anyone who stayed alive long enough to tell the story of the poor dead doofus' earthly departure.

James Brown Miller was born in Van Buren, Arkansas, on October 25, 1861. His parents, Jacob and Cynthia Miller, would eventually bring a total of nine children into the world. A year or two after Jim's birth, his father, for unknown reasons, moved the Miller clan to Franklin in Robertson County, Texas. Given the time and circumstances of the period, it probably had more than a little to do with the precarious and unsettled nature of trying to stay alive. This pesky problem was brought on by Civil War border ruffians, who spent most of their waking hours trying to see how many people they could rub off the face of the earth as they ripped through Kansas, Missouri, and Northern Arkansas.

Stories exist—and have often been repeated—that God gathered both Jim's parents to their heavenly reward while he was but a dirty-diapered child. This unfortunate event—our unsubstantiated story goes—caused him to be taken in by his grandparents. A few years later for unexplained reasons the old folks turned up extremely dead at their home in Evant, and at a very tender age—around eight according to the legend—young Mr. Miller was charged with the murders but never brought to trial. (Modern American hand wringers who think that our youthful man slayers are the only ones like them to ever commit such crimes should go back and read this passage at least

Formal portrait of Killin' Jim Miller as a young man. No trace can be detected of the hardened and vicious murderer he would become before being lynched on April 19, 1909. (Photo courtesy of Western History Collections, University of Oklahoma Libraries)

three times along with those previous pages that describe John Wesley Hardin's first four efforts at the butchery of his fellow man at age fourteen or fifteen.)

No real reason can be ascertained for this unlikely fable. It suffers considerably under the weight of a very simple fact—his mother still counted herself among the living when he actually did step across the line and commit a heinous crime on July 30, 1884. That act was considered so shocking that it got the full and undivided attention of every law enforcement type for miles around.

By that point in his life he had to have been around twenty-three years of age. Jim had lived with his sister Georgia and her husband, John Coop, for several years on Plum Creek, about eight miles northwest of Gatesville. Mr. Coop evidently harbored no compunction whatever when it came to applying the strap or his fists to young Mr. Miller if he felt it necessary for anything in the way of discipline. Young Jim resented the hell out of such treatment.

The definitive reasons for his actions on July 30 are not known and never will be, but we do have an absolutely clear picture of what he did. That afternoon he borrowed a shotgun from W.R. Basham—his uncle who lived nearby—then at about eight o'clock that night he crept up on his brother-in-law, who slept on the front porch because of the summer heat, and shot the man to death as he peacefully snoozed away.

When the law showed up, arrested him, dragged him to jail, indicted and put him on trial, Miller claimed to have been in the amen corner of a singing and shouting prayer meeting some three miles away from the Coop home at a place called Camp Branch. Prosecutors had a field day with his story. Miss Georgia Large, his date for the evening, testified that Jim did indeed attend the services with her but left shortly after the preaching began. Prosecutors got her to further admit that Miller didn't return until after the preacher finished up and the shouting started.

Lee Basham, his cousin, nailed the lid down when he bore witness that while on their way to the camp meeting earlier that afternoon, Miller had pretty clearly threatened Coop when he said something like, "I'm going to kill a fellow tonight." And as they made their way back home after the fellowship services and some home baked angel food cake, Jim even admitted to Basham that he'd accomplished his previously stated goal.

Miller's sister, the other Georgia, tried to save him with a story of brotherly affection between her husband and short-fused sibling, but no one on the jury bought it. They interpreted Lee Basham's recollection of Miller's mutterings as meaning, "I *am* going to kill a fellow tonight." Then they promptly found him guilty after the prosecution proved beyond a shadow of a doubt that he could have easily made it to the scene of the crime and back to the meeting on a good horse in the time described by his date, Miss Georgia Large.

Jim's conviction didn't matter a damned bit though. An appeals court reversed the decision, and the criminal justice system never bothered him with the matter again. The most obvious thing that came out of all this was the first recorded instance of a developing pattern used in much of his later behavior. Elements of the Coop model included a shotgun, an unsuspecting victim, murderous assault by way of stealth or from hiding, an attempted alibi that looked good on the surface, and a trial that went nowhere—even if a conviction resulted from his actions.

This same story got retold over and over for the rest of his life. He didn't seem to worry much about any of his murderous actions, for few if any eyewitnesses ever came forward to testify against him. Killin' Jim spent most of his waking moments from the death of his brother-in-law till he died either on trial, awaiting trial, or appealing conviction for his numerous deadly actions and other scrapes with the law.

About a year after her husband's death, Georgia Miller Coop passed away. Early in 1886 brother Jim drifted to San Saba County where he fell in with bad company, did a little cowboy type stuff, drank, gambled, and supposedly worked for a brief time as a Texas Ranger. An unsubstantiated legend has it that a

Interior of one of El Paso's favorite watering holes, the Senate Saloon as it appeared in 1881. City Marshal J.B. Gillett is seated second from the left. (Photo courtesy of Western History Collections, University of Oklahoma Libraries)

ranger named Jim Miller chased a desperado named Davenport into the unfriendly environs of Mexico and dragged him back to Texas for his just deserts. Some believe this was the same James B. Miller, although others maintain that no evidence exists that our own Killin' Jim was ever a Texas Ranger at that point in his life.

By 1887 Mannen Clements hired him ostensibly to herd, rope, and brand cattle—cowboy stuff. Most put absolutely no credit in that particular piece of blanket fuzz and feel his real talent involved providing another gun anytime the Clements clan needed one. While working for Papa Mannen, he and Clements' son Mannie became trail mates and close friends. He also fell in love with Mannie's sister Sarah Francis Clements, called Sallie, but kept that to himself. He evidently wanted the proper opportunity to come along so he could prove his loyalty to the clan. Given the time and circumstances, it didn't take long.

In March, Miller's mentor, Mannen, ran for sheriff of the newly formed Runnels County. During the campaign he pretty much let everyone who wanted to listen know just how he felt about the sorry politics of the area and his less than worthy opponent. On March 29, 1887, the elder Clements and Ballinger city marshal Joe Townsend got into a shoving and shouting match at the Senate Saloon. Pistols came out, and Joe Townsend sent Clements to that great cattle roundup in the sky with some well-placed shots to the chest.

A night or so after Papa Clements bit the dusty floor in the Senate, a shotgun blast from the dark knocked Marshal Townsend out of the saddle near his home. He managed to survive the assault but had to have his mangled left arm amputated and was never the same man after that. Although everyone within fifty miles knew Jim Miller did the shooting, he wasn't talking and there was no way to prove it because by the time Townsend dropped from the back of his horse to the ground, Miller had managed to turn up in Eddy/Carlsbad, New Mexico.

A year or so later, having proven his trustworthiness to the Clements family by sending the hated Townsend close enough to the edge of hell to smell the smoke, he married the lovely Sallie. Accompanied by his friend and now brother-in-law, Mannie, the newlyweds moved to the West Texas town of Alpine in Brewster County.

During their three-year stay in the dusty little burg, two things of note occurred. Jim and Sallie's first child, Carrie Brown Miller, was born but died in infancy, and the first instance of Miller's open solicitation of murder for hire occurred in the presence of a reliable source.

According to no less than famed Texas Ranger Jim Gillett, he sat in the chair of an Alpine barbershop one steamy afternoon when Miller opened the door, poked his head inside, and said quite plainly, "I hear tell somebody in Alpine wants Judge

Gillis killed. Pass the word I'll take the job for two hundred dollars." Historians who've examined the tale closely have left no record of whether he made good on his sales pitch or even who exactly Judge Gillis was for that matter. But the important thing for us to remember here is that he had the absolute flat-footed gall to offer such services in so open a manner. He might just as well have printed up handbills and tacked them on every wall and post in town.

In 1891 the Millers and their extended family retreated even further into the hinterlands when they landed in a gritty and grizzled West Texas town named Pecos. This move seems to have been precipitated by a murder, but not one committed by Killin' Jim. No, in this instance Mannie Clements was probably responsible for the death of Sam Taylor, and several pesky law enforcement dudes wanted to do some serious talking with him about it. A quick trip deeper into West Texas seemed like a good idea.

By the time they reached Pecos, civilization had begun to emerge in the area, but the Reeves County seat was still as rough and tumble a place as you could have found in Texas and very much on the edge of civilization even at that late date. Such raw, crude, and dangerous places still needed lawmen with more crust than an armadillo, who knew how to use a gun and had more grit than boiled eggs rolled in sand.

County Sheriff G.A. "Bud" Frazer fit the bill to a tee, but he was also a practical man and always on the prowl for some tough-as-nails help. He had his hands full with a crowd of rowdies who hung out in an area called "Dobie Town" over on the wrong side of the tracks. When Miller applied for a deputy sheriff's job, Frazer liked what he saw. He hired the tall intense man, drove him all over the county, and introduced his new lawdog to everyone who was anyone. Things seemed to be working out

Pecos, Texas, saloon scene taken in the late 1880s. The man seated at the table wearing the white hat is believed to be Killin' Jim Miller. (Photo courtesy of Western History Collections, University of Oklahoma Libraries)

about as well as Frazer could have ever hoped. My-oh-my but did he have a surprise coming or what?

Miller took rooms in a hotel across from the bank and could soon be seen entering and leaving the saloons, bars, dancehalls, and gambling houses on such a regular basis that some of the owners began to observe that he just might be a bit "too energetic." Most also noted that he never appeared on the scene except in the performance of his official duties, and he did not imbibe in *espiritus fermenti*, smoke or gamble, or keep company with floozies.

When that fall's revival services cranked up to full screech, Miller joined the church and could be found at every service on the deacon's bench amenin' like a man possessed. His impassioned religious activities made him popular with the "good" folk of Pecos, and because of his sober black attire and black

Stetson they just naturally started referring to him as "Deacon" Jim.

Everything went along swimmingly until cattle and horses started disappearing right and left. Miller spent days away from town on the rustling bastards trails (at least that's what he claimed) but never seemed able to catch them. As more and more animals vanished, he managed to get appointed hide and livestock inspector. This gave him authority to pursue the bandits outside Reeves County. Even that didn't help; in fact the situation just got worse as cows and horses continued to disappear at an alarming rate.

At a meeting called by local livestock owners to try and stop the hemorrhaging, Bud Frazer's brother-in-law, Barney Riggs, suggested that the best way to stop the thievery was to get rid of Jim Miller. Miller tried to laugh it off by noting that Barney might be right. The town quickly split into two highly opinionated groups—one that supported Miller and another that didn't.

Bud Frazer tried to avoid taking sides in the somewhat gnarly matter, but he did go back and investigate Deacon Jim's background for the first time, and he didn't necessarily like what he found. Miller's kinship, no matter how distant, with gunmen like Mannie Clements and John Wesley Hardin got Frazer to scratching his head. Such relations might not prove much, but they bore watching. So he refused those who requested the Deacon's dismissal. It would turn out to be the most fateful decision of his life and one he would live to regret.

A few weeks later Frazer assigned Jim the job of escorting a Mexican prisoner to Fort Stockton. The deputy sheriff and his captive left town together, but Miller returned a short time later and claimed that his ornery ward tried to escape and the Deacon found it necessary to kill the man.

Since no other witnesses came forward, Frazer was forced to accept Miller's version of the shooting. He should have gotten a hint as to Miller's attitude about the murder when Deacon Jim was later quoted as having said, "I have lost my notch stick on the number of Mexicans that I've killed out on the border." For those unfamiliar with a notch stick, his rather candid remark seems to indicate that he'd killed so many Spanish-speaking folks that he could no longer keep count of them.

At some point during all this talk, Barney Riggs came to his brother-in-law with a totally different version of why his deputy's prisoner had abruptly cashed in his tacos. He claimed, "The Mex knew where Miller disposed of a pair of dun mules south of the border." The Deacon's most vocal critic wouldn't give it up as to who told him the story, but Sheriff Frazer followed Barney's directions, found and recovered the mules, returned to Pecos, fired Miller, and even went so far as to charge him with theft of the animals. He probably knew it wouldn't stick and it didn't.

When elections rolled around that summer, an unemployed Killin' Jim—who was still madder'n a teased weasel—ran for office against Frazer but lost to the popular sheriff in a landslide. But, hey, did the pasting he got in a little ol' election keep a man like Miller down? Hell no! He went and got himself appointed city marshal, hired Mannie Clements on as one of his night deputies, and frequently kept company with gunfighters like Bill Earhart, John Denston, and M.Q. Hardin. Denston, his wife's cousin, enjoyed something of a killer's reputation in his own right.

In May 1893 Sheriff Frazer escorted some prisoners down to their new iron barred hotel in Huntsville. While he was thus occupied, Marshal Miller stepped back, threw up his hands, and all hell broke loose in Pecos. Thugs, drunks, and gunmen took over the streets. Decent citizens tried to run for cover but still managed to get beaten, robbed, and shot. Someone got word to

Texas Ranger Captain John R. Hughes helped Pecos County Sheriff G.A. "Bud" Frazer get the bulge on Pecos City Marshal Jim Miller during one of their numerous confrontations. Miller killed Frazer on September 14, 1896, while the ex-sheriff played poker with friends in a Toya, Texas saloon. This photo of the retired Hughes was taken on July 10, 1928, in El Paso. (Photo courtesy of Texas Ranger Hall of Fame & Museum - Waco, Texas)

the sheriff that his town was flying to pieces, and he hopped the next train home in what has been described as "a fighting rage."

Meanwhile over in one of "Dobie Town's" watering holes, a citizen named Con Gibson overheard M.Q. Hardin and some other less-than-saintly types as they discussed the hot reception planned for Frazer when he stepped off the train. Gibson, his singed ears still smoking, scorched the dusty streets of Pecos on his way to tell his brother James, the county clerk, what he'd overheard. They sent a telegram to Frazer that hit his hands on the Southern Pacific line's passenger train on its way back to Pecos. Bud enlisted the help of his friend Texas Ranger Captain John R. Hughes and one of his men.

The whole town got wind of the possible killing and elbowed its way up to the station to watch the entertainment as Frazer stepped off the train with a Texas Ranger at each elbow. Eyewitnesses said the would-be assassins abandoned the platform like a herd of turpentined cats. Others noted that Marshal Jim Miller's lower jaw dropped almost to the buckle on his gun belt. But he recovered quickly and tried to welcome Frazer with a handshake and a groveling statement that he sure was glad ol' Bud was back 'cause he needed some help with Pecos' unexplainable recent crime wave.

Frazer showed plenty of grit when he refused to take Miller's offered hand in full view of the whole town. The next day he had his Texas Ranger buddies arrest and throw the whole damned bunch in jail on a charge of conspiracy to murder him. Clements and Hardin made bond so fast Frazer's eyeballs must have been spinning in his head as they blew out of his office.

Killin' Jim wasn't as lucky as his fellow schemers. For whatever reason, the sheriff refused to let him back out on the streets. After considerable yelping from some of Miller's friends, they raised the money for his inflated bail, and Frazer eventually had to release him against his own better judgment.

All the frustrated potential murderers ended up on trial, and each swore as to his friend's love of the Lord and complete lack of understanding as to why they'd been accused of such heinous things. The courts did what could only be considered fairly typical of the time. They quashed the case against Miller and Clements. Hardin got a change of venue to El Paso where he was quickly acquitted. Bud Frazer had to stand by and watch as men who had plotted to kill him rode back into town like they owned it. All he could do was watch his back, make sure his pistols were loaded, and wait for the next move.

About the only good thing that came of the entire fracas involved Jim Miller being relieved of his city marshal's job. Most people breathed a sigh of relief and felt sure he'd leave town, at least most of them wished he would. Killin' Jim not only stayed in town, he went into the hotel business right under Bud Frazer's nose.

Meanwhile, Con Gibson's brother James made it clear that if Con stayed around Pecos, his life would be about as worthless as a four-card flush. Gibson hit the ground running and didn't stop till he got to Eddy/Carlsbad, New Mexico. There was a small problem though. He just didn't run far enough. A few days into his self-imposed exile, John Denston showed up and killed the hell out of him.

Back in Pecos Sheriff Frazer got word of his friend's untimely departure and knew beyond any shadow of a doubt that Con's death was a payback murder done to send Bud and his cohorts a ringing message. By that time almost everyone in town had seen and heard about all they ever wanted out of Jim Miller. The consensus was that the sooner he got the hell out of town the better. But if anyone really thought the man would do the right thing, they had another think coming. He not only stayed but also paraded around in his black frock coat like he'd been elected mayor.

On April 12, 1894, Miller strutted out the door of his hotel and stopped a few feet off his front porch to talk with a friend. They swapped a few lies and generally jawed around until Sheriff Frazer strolled up, pistol drawn, and said, "Here's one for Con Gibson!" His first shot hit Miller dead center and bounced off the man's chest! Frazer was stunned to say the least. But he kept his head and put his second slug in Miller's right arm as the former marshal tired to draw his own weapon. Badly wounded, Jim reached behind his back with his left hand, drew his gun, and finally started pitching some of his own lead.

Chapter 4

About the only thing his wrong-handed effort managed to do was put a large hole in the single bystander who witnessed the fight. Storekeeper Joe Kraus heard the first shot and got to the boardwalk in front of his mercantile just in time to go down when Miller's second piece of wild lead hit him in the hip.

Sheriff Frazer kept up a steady barrage of fire. He sent three more into Jim's chest, but to his amazement the man kept coming. Finally his last slug went low and hit the Deacon just above the belt line and punctured his diaphragm. By all the unwritten rules of killing, Jim Miller should have been dead, dead, dead and ready for the undertaker.

A rattled Bud Frazer stumbled back to his office, certain that he'd never have to deal with that pesky problem again. Some of Miller's cronies scooped him up and carried him off the bloody street. They rushed him back inside the hotel where they discovered that three of the sheriff's well-placed shots covered an area about the size of a ten-dollar gold piece just over Killin' Jim's heart. Beneath his shredded shirt and coat rested a piece of steel plate that had protected him from his assailant's deadly salvo of .45 long Colt slugs.

Once again the town split right down the middle over who had the right in the matter. Many felt Miller was a weasel, but hell, Bud shouldn'a just walked up and started shooting like that without giving the man a fair chance. Still others wondered aloud why the sheriff didn't shoot ol' Jim in the head. John Wesley Hardin would have, and hell, that would'a settled the whole thing once and for all.

By the time elections were held in July, the county's entire population got to figgerin' that everyone would be better off if they could get some relief from the bad blood. A man named Daniel Murphy ran against Sheriff Frazer and won. Miller endorsed the new man from his sickbed. That probably wasn't worth a hell of a lot, but it swung enough weight to put Frazer on the streets, and that was exactly what the Deacon wanted.

The defeat took a terrible toll on Bud Frazer. The former ranger's family could trace its roots to the earliest settlements in West Texas, and rejection by his friends and neighbors was almost more than he could bear. Not long after Dan Murphy's swearing-in ceremony, the now unemployed sheriff packed his bags, put all his Pecos property up for sale, and headed west.

Once his wounds healed sufficiently, Killin' Jim strutted around town and bragged that he had tied a can to Frazer's tail and would finish the job the first time he got a chance. He even made several trips into New Mexico in an effort to try and make good on his threats and went all the way to Lordsburg but couldn't find the former sheriff. He needn't have worried. Fate always seems to have a way of making things happen if you want them bad enough.

In December 1894, almost two years after the first gunfight, Frazer returned to Pecos to finalize the sale of some property. By accident the two men met near Zimmer's blacksmith shop. Heavy-duty blasting commenced forthwith.

For Pecos' former favorite lawman, it must have seemed like déjà vu all over again. He beat Miller to the draw and put one in Deacon's right arm and another in his left leg faster'n God could get there. But the man still wouldn't go down. Miller sprayed lead all over town with his left hand again, and Bud's well-placed shots once more bounced off Jim's chest plate.

Bud Frazer was one of those men who would probably have walked into hell with no more than a switch to defend himself, but his inability to put Miller on his back must have shaken the man right to the soles of his boots. After he bulls-eyed ol' Jim several more times, he turned and ran for his life.

Friends, who were getting pretty good at this by now, rushed out and picked Miller up again. From his bloody bed the

Deacon swore out a warrant for assault with intent to do murder on his person, and Bud Frazer's replacement was forced to arrest Pecos' popular ex-sheriff.

In March 1895 a Reeves County grand jury indicted their former lawman, but the judge decided there wasn't a chance in hell of him getting a fair trial anywhere around Pecos and ordered a change of venue to El Paso County.

Miller retained his wife's distant cousin John Wesley Hardin as a special attorney for the prosecution—whatever that was, or is. The old gunfighter had recently arrived in the Pass City after having spent over fifteen years in the State Prison at Huntsville. But his notoriety didn't help Miller's cause much. The jurors couldn't agree on a verdict, so Judge Buckler discharged them on April 14, 1895, and set a new trial date for May '96 in Colorado City.

About four months later on August 19, 1895, Hardin made the mistake of turning his back on John Selman in the Acme Saloon and paid for that little slip-up with his life. He probably wouldn't have been of much help to Deacon Jim the second time around anyhow. On May 20, 1896, a jury of twelve good men and true from Mitchell County, who didn't know Miller or his sanctimonious ways, decided that he got just about what he deserved in his disagreement with Frazer and acquitted Bud.

For about three months they managed to stay as far away from one another as they could. Most folks who'd been shot four times by the same man would wisely make it a point to avoid a bad boy like Frazer no matter what it took. Not Killin' Jim. He kept track of Frazer's every move through friends who acted as a network of spies all over West Texas and most of New Mexico.

Bud didn't act foolish or take any chances. He bought himself a specially built pistol that fired *explosive* loads designed to blow a man in half.

A realistic Barney Riggs reportedly told his brother-in-law, "Be careful. Miller may never give you a chance to use it." The man should have been a prophet.

On the night of September 13, 1896, Bill Earhart hooked up with Miller just outside Pecos. He brought two horses for each man and they rode the hell out of them to get to a hotel room in Toya. Miller had it on pretty good authority that Frazer now spent much of his free time gambling in the saloon directly across the street. The front door of the little home for wayward cowboys was easily viewed from his hotel window.

The next morning Earhart strolled down to the saloon and took a seat while Deacon Jim watched all the comings and goings from his second floor perch. At exactly nine o'clock Bud entered and took the seat Earhart offered at a table with Johnson Tate, Andy Cole, and J.E. Jerrell. Any suspicion Frazer might have harbored by being guided into a seat facing the door by a known supporter of Miller's like Earhart must have been allayed when the Pecos gunman pulled up another chair and sat down with them as a spectator. Bartender Pat Flowers and a Toya local named J.D. Shelton picked their teeth and watched. Earhart might have been the only one in the room who knew it, but everything was in place for the climax of a tragic play.

Apparently his crony somehow signaled Miller when everything was properly staged for his appearance. Problem is no one could explain exactly how he managed to accomplish that without being spotted. Anyway, Bud's behind had barely hit the seat of his greasy chair when Miller charged across the street, shotgun in hand. Everyone in attendance except Earhart would later swear that they hadn't seen or heard anything out of the way until a double-barreled shotgun blast from the doorway almost turned their eardrums into mush.

Andy Cole would testify that Frazer's chair was about nine feet from the door when the first shot was fired. Another witness said that the two barrels of buckshot practically removed Bud's head from his body. His exact words were, "I saw his whole head disappear in a clot of splashing blood and bone."

Frazer's sister got word of his death and rushed to her brother's side. Weeping profusely, she threw herself across his body and tried to find his pistol, but someone had taken it. Distraught, she tried to get the bartender to give her a gun. He refused. She ran back home, armed herself, and accompanied by her mother, managed to get back to Pecos at almost exactly the same second as Miller.

The sister got the drop on him, but cool as cucumbers at a tea party the Deacon said, "If you try to use that gun, I'll give you what your brother got—I'll shoot you right in the face!" Well that slowed the proceedings down a bit, but the Frazer girl stood her ground and gave Miller a public tongue lashing said to have been unparalleled in the history of blue language. Years later witnesses shook their heads when they recalled the blistering she delivered. Ol' Jim waited till she finished then told her to take all the other Frazers and Barney Riggs and get out of Reeves County or die.

Well if he thought he'd thrown a scare into Barney Riggs he had another think coming. Riggs got back to Toya from a trip to Fort Stockton and learned from his wife of Earhart and Miller's complicity in the murder of his relative and close friend along with the threats against his own life. With no hesitation, he checked the loads in his pistol, took his saddle off one horse, threw it on another, and headed for Pecos in a dead run.

He arrived in town ready for a fight only to find that he couldn't get at Miller. Sheriff Murphy already had the Deacon in jail. So he rumbled around town and stumbled into the Orient Saloon where Earhart and John Denston had spent the morning downing a few dippers of joy juice. Words flew in both directions, and Earhart came up fastest, but Barney ducked and his return shot caught Miller's cohort smack between the eyes.

Denston made the mistake of needing a gun and not having one that day. He tried to get the pistol from his dead friend's hand, but fear overcame him. He headed for the door and the hoped-for safety of the street. Didn't work! Riggs followed him, coolly took aim, and put a bullet in the back of Denston's skull that splattered head filler, bone, blood, and teeth all over the street.

In his book *Shotgun for Hire* Glenn Shirley reported that a man named Mark Mitchell, a close friend of Denston's victim Con Gibson, picked a gob of Denston's brains out of the dust. When asked what in the hell he could possibly want with them, he reportedly said he intended to send them to Con's widow in Comfort, Texas.

Sheriff Murphy arrested Barney. He immediately posted bond and spread the word around Pecos that the country wasn't big enough for him and Miller, so he figured he'd just have to kill the Deacon the next time he saw him. A grand jury indicted him for pulling Earhart and Denston up by the roots. His trial ended in El Paso on May 18, 1897, with an acquittal in what the jury described as a "clear-cut case of self-defense." Those twelve good men went out just long enough to write down two words and come back in—"not guilty."

By the time Barney got back home, Miller's friends had persuaded him to head 'em up and move 'em out. Mannie Clements probably made the most convincing argument when he pointed out that the Deacon's breastplate wasn't worth a damn against a man like Barney Riggs. Hell, he'd shoot you in the head, for crying out loud!

For once in his life Deacon Jim Miller decided to take some good advice. Indicted for the shotgun murder of Bud Frazer, he again managed to get a change of venue. This time the site of

Emanuel "Mannie" Clements was John Wesley Hardin's cousin and Jim Miller's brother-in-law by marriage. He is shown here standing on the steps of his home in El Paso, Texas. (Photo courtesy of Western History Collections, University of Oklahoma Libraries)

his trial was a little frontier town of less than a thousand souls named Eastland near Fort Worth. He moved his family there in early December of '96. His naturally temperate disposition and churchgoing ways soon made him popular with all the good people of the windblown little railroad town. He even took a job managing a hotel and never missed a prayer meeting just to keep a good face on a bad situation.

When his case came to trial in June 1897, people are rumored to have come from all over Texas to watch. The *Fort Worth Register* complained that all the bad men you could have rounded up between the Pecos River and El Paso showed up. A troop of special deputies and Texas Rangers were brought in to give the local lawdogs some help just in case anything wayward chanced. But nothing did, and the Deacon's lawyers called a whole slew of his Pecos running buddies who swore to his exemplary character and previous injuries at the hands of former Sheriff Frazer. Johnson Tate and Pat Flowers refuted the negative testimony of Cole, Jerrell, and Shelton by declaring that Jim Miller was a saint and had acted exactly the way any member of the jury would have. Hell, boys, it was self-defense as sure as the cow ate the cabbage.

In spite of that astonishing pile of bull feathers, the jury hung on a vote of 11 to 1 for conviction, and the judge ordered a new trial for January of '99. Between hearings Miller traveled around the countryside with a circuit preacher holding prayer meetings, and when his second trial finally came up, the jury acquitted him because, they said, he didn't do anything any worse than Frazer had. Except maybe kill the man, something they conveniently forgot.

No sooner had the verdict passed the jury foreman's lips than Deacon Jim went right back to his old tricks. He bought half interest in a local saloon—on credit no less—then pretended to leave town. During his absence his new partner made the mistake of taking a buggy ride in the woods with Sallie Clements Miller. He got word pretty quick that Killin' Jim knew about his afternoon tryst with his wife. The new partner promptly vanished and left the Millers with sole ownership of a West Texas cantina that they immediately put on the market. The ink had barely dried on the bill of sale when they hotfooted it for Memphis, a major cattle shipping point about a hundred miles southeast of Amarillo.

Miller hadn't been in town long when the body of a prominent cattleman named William Janes of Old Elm Creek turned up riddled with a load of buckshot that had also removed most his head. Think for a second; sounds kinda familiar doesn't it?

Someone put up a $10,000 reward for the arrest and conviction of the lowlife murderin' scum who put Bill Janes in the ground. John Beasley, a local tax assessor, was indicted for the murder on the word of a Miller associate named Joe Earp. Earp swore he'd seen Beasley riding away from the Janes farm just after he heard gunshots on the afternoon of January 16, 1898. Everyone in the area knew of longstanding feuds between Janes and several other area families. His death stayed in the unsolved column until Earp came forward with his fanciful story that did wonders toward guiding any inquiries about Deacon Jim in another direction—this in spite of the fact that few people could be found who actually believed Earp.

Joe's tale of witnessed murder fell apart like a paper suit in a rainstorm when Beasley's lawyers proved that he had been in Eastland testifying on behalf of his close friend Jim Miller the day he claimed to have heard the shots and seen the innocent tax assessor near the Janes place. Shucks and wazoo! Some major legal type stuff started flying though the air in North Texas!

The court immediately dismissed the case against Beasley, charged Earp with perjury and Killin' Jim with subornation of perjury. In an effort to save his own hide, Earp turned state's evidence and admitted that the story he'd told on Beasley was a lie and that Miller had arranged the entire episode in order to collect that handsome $10,000 reward on a murder the Deacon had most likely committed himself. Earp's damning testimony raised the specter of Miller's deep involvement in the Old Elm Creek feud and his overt participation in the plot to assassinate Janes.

On August 11, 1898, plans existed for a man named Jarrett Nelson to testify against Miller. Everyone believed that his statement would identify the Deacon as the triggerman in the Janes murder. But Nelson never made it to the courtroom in Wellington. Someone (let's all put our thinking caps on here and see if we can guess who) put so much daylight in Nelson's hide you could have read the *Fort Worth Register* through it. Miller and several of his friends were immediately charged and indicted for the murder.

All the cases against Killin' Jim got transferred to another court in Wilbarger County, and faster'n double greased lightning they all got dismissed—except the one for subornation of perjury. He went to trial for that one, and a jury actually convicted him of the crime on October 3, 1901. But hey, did it matter even the least little bit? Hell no! Two months later the findings were reversed and the case dismissed! Killin' Jim Miller was loose on the public once again, and he was—to put it mildly—madder'n a rooster in an empty hen house.

Most of his ire was reserved for former friend and cohort Joe Earp. Jim'd had to spend all the time from his conviction to reversal on the subornation charge in jail. Upon his release he'd told reputable witnesses on the train home that they could watch the newspapers for Earp's upcoming obituary. Three weeks later *someone* ambushed ole Joe in Coryell County and killed him deader'n Julius Caesar's buddy Brutus. Judge Charles

Chapter 4

Brice had heard Miller make the threat but told no one about it until years later for fear he might just join Joe Earp in cold storage.

The Deacon's prosecutor in the Janes case, J.M. Standlee, got sick and mysteriously died a horrible death not long after Miller's conviction got reversed. Years later the doctor who examined Standlee's corpse and listed the cause of death as peritonitis admitted the lawyer had actually died of a heavy-duty case of arsenic poisoning. The doctor checked around shortly after Standlee's hasty exit from this life and discovered the hotel's regular cook hadn't shown up the night the doomed prosecutor came down ill. The cook's stand-in turned out to be another Miller associate who disappeared the day the poisoned Mr. Standlee got pronounced deceased. As had been the case with Judge Brice, the good doctor kept this story to himself for fear he'd end up just as dead as the arsenic-laced lawyer.

Miller smiled all the way to his new home in Fort Worth. In 1901 he moved into a residence at 500 East Sixth Street and claimed to be a real estate agent. He and his wife lived there for about three years. During that time his business kept him out of town for lengthy periods of time.

It's a pretty safe bet most of those trips didn't involve the sale of anything other than services rendered for ambush killings done. Rumors exist that Miller went into the murder for hire trade on a fairly large scale and did it all from the comfort of his favorite armchair in Fort Worth's Delaware Hotel.

Sheepherder and cattleman disputes had flared up again after having died down in the 1880s. The cattle-raising contingent of the early 1900s often found itself in need of the services easily purchased from a man like Miller. In the midst of all his previous scrapes with the law, unsolved murders in the Killin' Jim vein continued being done in virtually every corner of the state. Many of his absences from the Fort Worth scene between

1901-1904 probably involved the fulfillment of contracts that required rubbing out anyone the Deacon got paid to blast into kingdom come.

The going price for a dead sheep man was $150. Killer Miller bragged that he'd personally eliminated at least a dozen *men* and so many sheepherders and Mexicans he'd completely lost count. His lucrative murder for hire business would probably have gone on unabated if he hadn't gotten so greedy and mixed in with a stupid land grab deal.

In 1904 a detective for the American Freehold Land and Mortgage Company named T.D. "Frank" Fore helped bring criminal charges against Miller and some of his other friends in the "real estate" business for conspiring to forge land titles. By then Jim and his wife had moved to 309 Rusk Street, and he ran the Exchange Livery Stable as a front for his other endeavors.

Reports exist that Fore, a former deputy United States marshal, developed some kind of irrational hatred for Miller and seemed intent on bringing the man down anyway he could. Such feelings aren't really all that hard to understand: Miller made a life of breaking every law in the book, and Fore had spent most of his life trying to enforce them. Well versed in the use of guns, the former marshal was openly hostile toward Miller and was said to have publicly threatened the Deacon with an early departure from life on the Fort Worth scene anytime he got a chance.

The whole angry affair between the two finally came to an ugly head on March 10, 1904, in the men's washroom of Jim's favorite hangout, the Delaware Hotel. According to eyewitnesses (read cattlemen and personal friends of Jim Miller here), the final dustup was Fore's fault. The shooting occurred at about nine o'clock that morning after the Deacon followed Fore into the washroom and shot the man once in the left breast and again in the left hand. A number of men close to Miller offered testimony that Fore drew first and got what he deserved.

No mention was made of what Fore was doing in the washroom when he managed to get rudely shot—twice. At least one person claimed to have seen Fore with a pistol in his hand as he fell, but the very real possibility exists that it could have been something else. Whether justified or not, almost everyone agreed that Fore had threatened Miller on several previous occasions and would probably have lived longer if he'd kept his big mouth shut.

Gun smoke still floated in the air at the Delaware when Miller strolled down to the sheriff's office and gave himself up. He posted bond of $2,000 and walked before the day was over. Poor ol' Frank took his time dying. He was moved to a room on the ground floor of the hotel and finally cashed in his chips at 10:50 p.m. the night of March 13. Stricken family members surrounded him as he passed.

On May 4, 1906, a Fort Worth jury took only fifteen minutes to exonerate Deacon Jim in the shooting of Frank Fore. They did this in spite of his well-known reputation for a wagonload of dubious corpses he'd left in places all over the state. A few days after his release, someone used the Killin' Jim method and took a shot at him from ambush but only managed to put a hole in his new Stetson. Seems God had other plans for the man.

The ink had barely dried on his acquittal two months later when he shotgunned Deputy U.S. Marshal Ben Collins near Emet in the Indian Territory on the night of August 1, 1906. It took some serious detective work before the final version of what happened came to light. Seems a man named Clint Pruitt hired Miller to kill Collins because the deputy put a slug in his brother, Port Pruitt, that turned ole Port into a chair riding cripple. The Pruitt family swore bloody revenge and let it be known far and wide that they would eventually get Collins for what he'd done.

Miller was arrested, indicted, and spent some time in a Tishomingo jail awaiting judgment. But as happened so often in the past, conspirators died, witnesses disappeared, and the whole legal action against him fell apart. Late in 1907, with no prospect for a trial anytime in the near future, the judge on the case granted him bail, and Killin' Jim headed back to Fort Worth.

Legend has it that when he got back home from the Indian Territory, messages from brother-in-law Mannie Clements waited. Mannie, who now served as a constable in El Paso, advised that their relative, Carl Adamson, required the Deacon's deadly presence in Las Cruces, New Mexico. The story goes that Miller's most famous victim had been selected. His name was Pat Garrett, and the going price for turning the notorious lawman into coyote bait was $1,500—ten times more than your average sheepherder.

Major differences of opinion exist as to whether Deacon Jim Miller could actually claim responsibility for Garrett's death or not. No doubt about it Patrick Floyd Jarvis Garrett had beaucoup enemies, and a sizable number of them would have given a tub full of money to see him in the ground. Most of the folks who were just folks still hated him for what they deemed an ambush killing of dirty little Billy. But his problems with the citizens of Las Cruces seemed to have started with the mysterious disappearance on February 1, 1896, of Colonel Albert Jennings Fountain and his eight-year-old son Henry near White Sands, New Mexico. At the time Col. Fountain served as chief investigator and prosecutor for the Southeastern New Mexico Stock Grower's Association. A $20,000 reward—the largest in western criminal history—for the arrest and conviction of those responsible and retrieval of the bodies lit Pat up like a

Christmas tree. He got himself appointed to the vacant office of sheriff of Doña Anna County, investigated the incident, and arrested Oliver Lee, Jim Gilliland, Bill McNew, and Bill Carr in 1898. Big dollar signs must have been floating in his eyes. Everyone went to trial, except Carr, and all were acquitted in June of 1899. From then on the whole bunch had a serious axe to grind for Sheriff Garrett.

Then in October of the same year Pat and his deputy were involved in a shooting at the W.W. Cox ranch that resulted in the death of a fugitive known as Billy Reed. Reed died in a hail of gunfire while in the presence of Cox's pregnant wife. Mrs. Cox promptly miscarried her unborn child as a result of the ensuing agitation and W.W. got added to a growing list of people in New Mexico who wanted the lawman dead.

Anyway, after all this stuff had festered around on people's minds for more than ten years, the now former lawman found himself once again looking into the Fountain vanishing and in a land dispute with a tenant on his ranch named Wayne Brazel. Brazel had moved a herd of goats onto range Garrett felt should be reserved for cattle. When he found out about all those bearded woollies chewing up his grass, Pat was enraged.

Carl Adamson, a relative of Jim Miller's by marriage, in the guise of peacemaker arranged for Garrett and Brazel to meet on the road near Garrett's ranch and proceed to Las Cruces. There they were to rendezvous with a prospective real estate agent, who supposedly could settle the dispute between the two angry men by leasing the Garrett ranch and purchasing the hated goats. Most folks hold that the mysterious real estate agent was none other than Killin' Jim.

On February 29, 1908, about four miles outside town at a spot now believed to be near the Las Cruces Country Club, Adamson stopped the buggy in which he and the famed former lawman rode and walked to a spot in front of the team to relieve

Famed lawman credited with killing Billy the Kid, Pat Garrett may or may not
have been murdered for money by Jim Miller. It all depends on what you choose
to believe. (Photo courtesy of Western History Collections, University of
Oklahoma Libraries)

himself. He claimed later that the other two men, since they first met that morning, had been and continued heatedly arguing. At some point during Carl's personal twa-lett, Garrett climbed down himself and went to the rear of the buggy with the seeming intent of following the other man's lead—so to speak. And that's where everything got weird as hell.

Garrett and Brazel kept yammering at one another, and all of a sudden Adamson was shocked and amazed when gunshots rent the clear New Mexico air. He turned just in time to see Garrett hit the dirt like a hundred pound sack of chicken feed and Brazel still sitting on his horse, the legendary smoking pistol in hand. They covered the extremely dead Mr. Garrett with a robe and proceeded on to Las Cruces where Brazel surrendered himself to a local deputy sheriff named Felipe Lucero.

Virtually every word of testimony about Pat Garrett's demise pointed directly to Wayne Brazel, including the voluntary confession of guilt in the shooting he freely and frequently repeated before, during, and after a trial that resulted in his acquittal—*acquittal*, for crying out loud! Very simply put, no one believed a word Wayne Brazel said. To a man everyone within five hundred miles of the Garrett murder all felt him *incapable* of the killing. And because they felt him incapable of such a heinous deed, they let him go and believed whatever the hell they wanted to.

Captain Fred Fornoff of the Territorial Mounted Police and a close personal friend of Garrett's always felt Jim Miller did the dirty deed. He even went so far as to conduct his own personal investigation of the murder scene and did wonders in the way of justifying anyone who believed Brazel could not have done the killing.

Just off the road, Fred found a spot trampled down by a horse that he felt waited there for some time. Under a bush a short distance away he managed to locate two .44 Winchester shell casings. He posited that the real killer hid behind the bush and fired the first shot that hit Garrett in the back of the head and exited over his right eye. As the dying former lawman fell and rolled over, Brazel put another slug in Garrett's stomach.

Fornoff caused the mystery to deepen further when he spread the word that Miller had been seen conducting what the captain deemed mysterious business in White Oaks, Tularosa, San Augustine Pass, and Las Cruces just prior to the murder. As far as he was concerned Adamson and Miller's criminal backgrounds and close family ties were all the proof he needed that Garrett's death resulted from a high-level conspiracy that went a lot deeper than anyone really wanted to dig. Governor George Curry later wrote of Fornoff's findings that the only things that kept the true identities of those responsible for Garrett's death from being exposed were a lack of available secret service investigators and adequate funding.

Finally, New Mexico attorney general James M. Hervey kept the investigation of Garrett's death going for some time after the story had pretty well shaken out to what we have available to us today. He even went so far as to make a trip to Chicago and interview an old friend of Pat's named Emerson Hough. Hough had some pretty blunt advice for Hervey concerning the Brazel-Garrett business.

"Jimmy," he said, "Garrett got killed trying to find out who killed Colonel Fountain, and you'll get killed trying to find out who killed Garrett if you don't go home and forget the whole thing." There's every indication Hervey knew good advice when he got it.

By the time of Brazel's trial—and while the investigation into the Garrett murder proceeded apace—Deacon Jim had made it back to Fort Worth and resumed his comfortable overstuffed chair down at the Delaware Hotel. He didn't know it, but his string had almost played out.

In early 1909 Killin' Jim finally took the contract that caused the lid on his own personal cookie jar to get slammed shut and sealed tight. Oklahoma ranchers B.B. Burrell, Jesse West, and Joe Allen sought Miller's expertise in dealing with a prickly thorn in their collective grubby paw named Allen Augustus "Gus" Bobbitt. The feuding factions had been at each other's throats since the earliest days of Ada, Oklahoma's, settlement and involved disagreements over property and disputes over liquor sales and missing livestock.

Murder and threatened mayhem became so commonplace that the public was about to get all it could stand of the situation. Bobbitt pulled out of the Canadian River liquor trade and tried to confine himself to his cattle business. But the situation only got worse, and when West and Allen showed up on the streets of Ada gunning for Bobbitt, the public at large popped its collective cork. Under intense pressure Allen and West got out of the liquor business and moved their cattle operations to Hemphill County, Texas.

If Gus Bobbitt thought that was the end of his problems with the Allen-West bunch he was wrong. They nursed their wounded pride and patiently waited for the proper opportunity for revenge to present itself. Then all of a sudden everywhere cattlemen met, the conversations buzzed with stories of Pat Garrett's induction into that great lawman's hall of fame in the sky. Evidently his newly acquired inability to breathe led West and Allen to decide that Deacon Jim Miller was exactly what they needed to solve an old but still irritating pimple on their combined behinds.

Toward the end of February locals saw a tall, pinch-faced man in a long black frock coat and black Stetson moving through a wooded area near former Deputy U.S. Marshal Bobbitt's home a few miles south and west of Ada.

A few days later, on the evening of Saturday February 27, 1909, a short distance from his ranch house, Bobbitt and his neighbor Bob Ferguson rode home after a trip to Ada to purchase cottonseed meal cakes. According to Ferguson, a man who shielded his face passed them on a dun horse. Strapped behind his saddle and wrapped in a rain slicker was a shotgun. As the two wagons continued on and passed a wooded hollow about half a mile from Bobbitt's home, a shotgun blast from the trees hit the unsuspecting rancher in his lower extremities. As he jumped backward in reaction to the attack, a second shot tore into his left side and knocked him from the wagon.

Shortly after the murderous assault, Ferguson spotted the stranger on the dun horse as he left the cover of the trees and rode away. The wounded rancher managed to stay alive for almost an hour.

Gus Bobbitt's wife was summoned to the scene of the shooting and according to his wishes lay beside him on the ground and tenderly placed her head in his lap. He refused to unbutton his coat in an effort to spare his wife seeing the terrible wound in his side. During the short time he had left, he spoke lovingly to her, gave instructions as to how he wanted his property handled, made out a will, and gave a detailed description of his assassin. He admitted to his wife that he didn't recognize the man but made it clear he believed old and well-known enemies had hired the killer. He died about an hour after the shooting. A.A. "Gus" Bobbitt was buried in Ada's Rosedale Cemetery. Forty-two years later his wife, Tennie, was placed in the ground beside him.

When news got back to town of the cowardly murder of one of their leading citizens, an irate pack of folks from Ada went into high gear searching for the man responsible. In their opinion being shot down in a face-to-face gunfight was one thing, dying at the hands of a back-shooting coward could not be tolerated. The morning following Bobbitt's death, thousands of people beat the bushes and pursued the killer. They tracked the dun horse to a ranch rented by Miller's nephew, John Williamson. When he claimed not to know what the hell was going on, they beat the tar out of him till he told the mob his uncle, Jim Miller, rode the horse.

Dropped wire cutters discovered along the trail and used to get through fences as the killer made his way to Ada over backcountry pastures were traced to B.B. Burrell, who came back to town to make sure Miller got the right man. By the time the posse uncovered all this, their prey had already made it back to Texas. A telegram to Fort Worth resulted in the arrest of Deacon Jim and Burrell on March 30. Miller didn't resist and told the deputies who took him into custody that he would never give a peace officer trouble because—"I prefer to take my chances in court." Jesse West got fingered as Miller's employer. He and Joe Allen were brought to heel like cur dogs in Oklahoma City on April 8. Then the whole bunch got unceremoniously dragged back to Ada for what was cooking up to be a real short trial.

Judge H.J. Brown conducted preliminary hearings on April 15. Feelings ran so hot against the four conspirators he had to have his marshals search everyone before they were allowed to enter the packed courtroom. Killin' Jim's reputation preceded him like a dead elephant's two-week-old carcass lying in front of Judge Brown's bench. Everyone in Oklahoma knew of the Deacon's numerous murders, frequent acquittals, and how witnesses against him often vanished or got mysteriously dead. Word also spread pretty quickly in Ada that Miller counted a number of wealthy Texas and New Mexico cattlemen friends in his corner, who would work diligently to get him off again.

According to whispered stories, the gentleman thug knew too much about numerous previous assassinations. Most people believed there were those in the Texas/New Mexico cattleman contingent who feared Jim. Those same men felt he would spill his guts about who paid for those killings when the crunch came if they didn't get behind him with sterling testimonials and plenty of cash. But even that didn't help the Deacon with Bobbitt's murder. Sometimes fate steps up and puts an end to all the yammering and speculation. It happened this time—with deadly results.

At about 2 a.m. on the morning of April 19, 1909 a sizable crowd of masked Ada, Oklahoma citizens decided Jim Miller had escaped punishment for his crimes for the last time. A mob that has been described as having been comprised of anywhere from fifteen to two hundred fine, upstanding folks stormed the tiny local power company and shut off the electricity and telephone service to the entire town.

As soon as everything was dark, quiet, and unable to communicate with the outside world, the vigilantes hotfooted it over to the jail. They easily overwhelmed the two sleepy-eyed guards with some meticulously applied pistol barrels to their skulls before the poor goobers could even think of putting up a fight. Allen, West, Burrell, and Jim Miller were rudely dragged from their cells for what they had to have immediately known was a sure-fire hanging.

Jesse West fought his attackers like a cornered rat and got a terrific beating for his trouble. The other three men offered little or no resistance. Witnesses testified later that Miller was the only one to speak. "If you're gonna hang me, do it quick," he grumbled. All were roughly dragged to the Frisco Livery Stable on Townsend where four ropes dangled from the rafters.

The crowd wasn't *completely* heartless in the matter. They gave each man an opportunity to confess his sins against his fellow man and get right with God. Newspaper accounts quoted only one speaker. The much-abused Jesse West is reported to have said, "We don't know who you are and don't care. For myself, I know if I had a six-shooter, a few of you would bite the dust. But that's just talk as long as my shootin' iron is in Texas. You boys appear to have a job to do. Why don't you do it? We won't tell you anything, you sons-of-bitches."

That was about as much persuasion as the madder-than-hell citizens of Ada needed. They quickly put all the men but Miller to gurgling and swinging. For several minutes after his friends did the midair ballet, the mob "encouraged" the Deacon to confess and try for a little much-needed redemption.

All they got from him was, "Just let the record show that I've killed fifty-one men." He had to have been harder'n a railroad spike to make such a confession with death staring him in the face.

When it was glaringly obvious the Deacon's final jig was up, he handed a diamond ring to someone in the crowd and asked that it be delivered to his wife. Then he removed a diamond stud from the front of his shirt and requested they present it to his jailers for their kindnesses to him during his stay in their crude country lockup. He asked for his trademark black frock coat, but his request was refused. Some felt he still believed that as long as he wore that coat no harm could come to him.

A member of the mob jammed the Deacon's hat on his head. Miller laughed and calmly said, "I'm ready now, boys. You couldn't have killed me otherwise. Let'er rip!"

Well he got accommodated and damned quick. When the body finally stopped jerking and quaking a man stepped from the crowd, draped the notorious black coat over the shoulders of the remains of Deacon Jim Miller, and said, "It won't help him now."

About two hours later the sun got up enough for one of the most famous pictures ever taken of frontier justice at its most gruesome. It is said that the photographer snapped a second

This might well be the most famous photo of the lynching of a notorious gunfighter ever taken. It pictures Jim Miller shortly after his neck was stretched with co-conspirators Joe Allen, B.B. Burrell, and Jesse West. This piece of justice took place on April 19, 1909, in an abandoned Ada, Oklahoma, livery barn behind the jail. Miller dangles on the far left. (Photo courtesy of Western History Collections, University of Oklahoma Libraries)

shot but destroyed it. Before lunch that day the bodies were removed to the Walters Funeral Home to await being claimed by their families.

Sally Miller buried her husband in Fort Worth's Oakwood Cemetery. The pastor of the First Methodist Church, the Reverend H.D. Knickerbocker, conducted the interment services. An impressive piece of marble marks his final resting place, but the casual passerby could never guess from its appearance at the notoriety of the man buried there. The inscription reads simply, J.B. Miller—Oct. 25, 1861—Apr. 19, 1909—Husband.

Unlike John Wesley Hardin, the Deacon didn't grace us with a detailed retelling of his exploits in the murder trade. Many of the incidents that are frequently reused in newly penned versions of his life suffer somewhat from those old historical bugaboos of witness contradiction, unprovable facts, outright bull feathers, and—worst of all—the general passage of so many years after his death before anyone really gave a tinker's damn about who he was and what he did. Truth is we'll probably never know the truth about Deacon/Killin' Jim/Killer Jim Miller and just might be even more appalled than we are now if we could discover it.

After the folks in Ada decided his neck was too short and stretched it for him, his wife and children continued to live subdued, upright lives in Fort Worth. Sallie was eventually remarried to a Mr. Roy Redwine. When he passed away she moved back to the old family stompin' grounds of East Texas on a place near where John Wesley Hardin and the Clements clan laid the groundwork for reputations that have lasted over a hundred and fifty years.

She died on October 7, 1938, and was brought back to Fort Worth to be buried alongside her beloved first husband. The name carved into her stone simply reads Sarah Francis Miller. Some of Jim's children managed to make it till 1979 when the oldest son and only daughter died on the same day in June of that year. According to Bill James, writer of an excellent little biography named *Jim Miller: The Untold Story of a Texas Badman,* most of his descendants never knew anything about their notorious ancestor and that a good many probably still don't. But given the modern penchant for claiming a relationship to anyone who has even touched the sacred hem of fame, it should come as no surprise if there exists some who would jump at the opportunity to claim familial descent even from a man like Killin' Jim. Hell, everyone in Missouri, Arkansas, Tennessee, and Mississippi named James swears they're directly related to Jesse and Frank like it's a badge of glorified honor. As the sage once opined, life is certainly strange.

Chapter 5

Lampasas Legend

~━━━━━━━━━━━━━━━━━━~

Pink Higgins

In Bill O'Neal's *Encyclopedia of Western Gunfighters* and at least one other source document, John Calhoun Pinckney "Pink" Higgins is credited with having committed an act unparalleled in the realm of western shootings. Even a word of such grandiosity as "unparalleled" might not prove sufficient to properly describe, for the uninitiated, the exact impact of what might or might not have happened sometime in the summer of 1874 in an isolated area of Pink's West Texas ranch near the town of Lampasas.

Whilst scouting about one lovely semi-arid afternoon Pink came upon a lowlife, scurvy dog named Zeke Terrell. Terrell enjoyed the widespread reputation of being a well-known kemosabe of the infamous Horrell clan—a bunch of local Neanderthals roundly despised by the Higgins family for their admiration for other people's cattle. Rumor had it that the Zeker could chew tobacco off the Horrell plug anytime he wanted.

Hell, local folks believed Terrell and those Horrell boys were thicker'n feathers in a pillow.

As Pink climbed down off his cayuse and watched from a distance of approximately a hundred yards, Zeke put a rifle bullet into the brain of a Higgins cow. Then Zeke leaped from the back of his trusty steed and immediately went to gleefully butchering Pink's poor defenseless bovine.

Higgins' eyes must have pulled up about like BBs as he jerked his rifle from its scabbard and strolled about ten steps closer to his target to get a little better shot. He carefully aimed and from over two hundred fifty feet away took all the slack out of ol' Zeke's rope with a well-placed shot where the rustlin' bastard looked biggest. Terrell shook hands with that great cattle detective in the sky before his limp corpse hit the dusty ground.

Tenderfeet in the audience might imagine that, hell yes, dude, that was pretty bad. But, and this is a real big but, by the time Higgins reached the recently departed Señor Zeke, he was fit to be boiled down for glue. He grabbed his trusty bowie knife, finished Terrell's efforts at opening up the cow's abdominal cavity, pulled out all its greasy innerds, and stuffed ol' Zeke inside. A section of hide was cut into leather strips and used in a rough equivalent of stitching the beast back together with the rustler's feet still hanging outside. Had to have been a damned bloody and nasty afternoon's piece of work.

John Calhoun Pinckney "Pink" Higgins then climbed back on his horse and leisurely rode into town. Legend has it that upon his arrival he took his time as he gave the local sheriff a graphic accounting of the incident and finished with detailed directions to a spot where the lawman could find the most rare of all biological anomalies—a cow that died in its vain attempt to give birth to a thief! No doubt about it; that could have been a historic Kodak moment. Just imagine how often that picture would be reprinted today. Hell, bubba, you'd be looking at it right now—guaran-damn-teed.

Whether this story has one scintilla of truth in it—and there most certainly exist plenty of questions as to if it actually does—is really of little importance. What should be considered of real significance here is that at one point in the local history of Lampasas, Texas, Pink Higgins enjoyed a reputation powerful enough to support such a tale as this—legend or not.

Pink's parents brought him into this world on March 28, 1851, near Macon, Georgia. Three years later John and Hester Higgins struck out for Texas as part of a wagon train bound for Austin and the dream of a fortune to be made growing cotton. Three-year-old Pinckney retained no living memory of the arduous journey, but years later his father often reminded the entire family of the thirty-six prairie schooners in the wagon train and more than one hundred slaves that made up the company of bold pioneers.

Upon arrival in the wilds of Texas, the elder Higgins acquired some land near Austin and tried to raise cotton for a while, but the climate and rocky soil of the area couldn't support the venture. So in 1857 he decided to go into the cattle business and moved his family about eighty miles northwest of Austin into northeastern Lampasas County on the very edge of the frontier near a spot named Beehouse Creek.

At that point in time settlers of the area were very much on their own. No cavalry camped nearby to ride to their rescue, bugles blaring. And Comanches still freely roamed the countryside. Indian raids were commonplace over the entire region. Brutal murder, kidnappings, torture, theft, and arson grew so routine that after two years of exposure to such vagaries the elder Higgins once again found it necessary to shuffle his wife and five children to the safer climes of Bell County.

Boys grew up fast and hard as nails in those days. They quickly learned to ride, herd cows, break horses, and use deadly weapons of every type to protect themselves from enemies both real and perceived. Education consisted of little more than an intimate knowledge of the King James Bible primarily because they didn't have time for any formal schooling and such. John Higgins kept his sons busy doing a man's job of work from the first day they could tote, lift, chop, hoe, dig, or whatever else the old man could find for them to do.

After a sojourn of a few years in Bell County, the elder Higgins returned his family to Lampasas with the assistance of his oldest son. By then the total population of white folks had dwindled considerably, and they came back to an area with grazing a plenty and an abundance of available mustangs loose on the countryside. They also found a boatload of Native Americans who grew up in the belief that all those invading white devils were generously provided to them by the Great Spirit to be used specifically as targets.

The year was 1862, and the Comanche became bolder because of a decided lack of U.S. military types to help guard against the exact problems that had put the Higgins clan to packing and running in the first place. Cruel death at the hands of marauders had claimed the life of a fifteen-year-old boy named James Gacey a short time prior to the Higgins family's questionable return.

Gacey went out to round up some stock and ended up looking like granny's pin cushion and filled with rifle balls. The worst part of his unfortunate passing was that before his captors shot him full of arrows and other foreign objects, he was stripped naked, scalped, and turned into a running target.

Even after the Civil War ended and Federal troops occupied the state, between 1865 and 1867, more than 160 Texans met their fate at the hands of native peoples. As many as thirty were wounded and more than forty carried into captivity. When you consider the pitifully small population at the time, such figures must have had a huge impact. People often met fates so terrible as to be indescribable.

Almost every other family had at least one member who had been murdered, mutilated, or wounded in some horrific manner. No doubt about it, living in almost any part of West Texas at the time was tougher'n shovelin' sunlight and could be real short.

His youth kept him from taking part in the festivities back east during the Civil War, but during those early formative years the tough-as-a-boot-heel Pink frequently rode with posses that pursued those deemed renegade and was wounded on several different occasions. Years later he claimed to have fought the Comanche all over West Texas as a teenager.

When in pursuit, he and his friends and neighbors often traveled the rough countryside in the company of Tonkawas. The "Tonks" hated the Comanche for rooting them off their homeland and eagerly took part in any chase they felt would result in the death or destruction of their old enemies. They also practiced a form of cannibalism, and Pink reportedly witnessed this brutal and repellant custom on more than one occasion.

By the age of eighteen, Pink had joined a group called the Law and Order League. This loose-knit company of neighbors chased rustlers, fought Comanches, and meted out justice of the braided rope variety any by God time it was needed. Higgins seems to have adopted a deep and abiding hatred for those who liked to throw a wide loop, and it stayed with him for the rest of his life. Word got around pretty fast that anyone messin' with Higgins family property could expect something a lot worse than a woodshed lecture if son Pink caught you.

In 1868 the hard-boiled young Higgins accompanied a Lampasas local named Perry Townsen on a pioneering cattle drive to Wyoming. By the time he returned to Texas, Pink was a casehardened trail rider with ambitions of his own in the cattle herding business. For several more years he worked the herds of other men, but in 1872 he went in with Jasper Townsen, one of Perry's nephews, and Bob, Ben, and Alonzo Mitchell in an ambitious drive of 2,600 longhorns up the newly opened Western Trail to Dodge City, Kansas. Pink came back from Dodge with more money in his pocket than anyone from around Lampasas had ever seen and followed that stunning success with an even more ambitious push all the way to Kansas City. By the age of twenty-four the young Texan could boast of being a wildly successful trail boss and experienced buyer, seller, and trader of cattle and horses.

On January 1, 1875, he married Betty Mitchell May. Betty's first husband had died in November of 1871 and left her with an infant daughter. Pink met his future wife through her uncle Mack Mitchell and became close friends with another family member named Bill Wren. By the time Betty became pregnant with their second child, ol' Pink was eyeball deep in a death-dealing range war widely known as the Horrell-Higgins feud.

The Horrell tribe had been around the Lampasas area for about as long as the Higgins bunch. Sam Horrell moved his family from Arkansas in 1857 and took up residence on a ranch ten miles northeast of the frontier settlement. For some reason a few years after the Civil War old Sam and his crew decided to move to California. They rounded up a herd and managed to get as far as Las Cruces, New Mexico, before the bottom fell out of their washtub.

While acting in his role as trail boss, brother John was impolitely shot dead by a drover who claimed that the stingy bastard hadn't paid him since they left Texas. Then in January 1869 the dead man's widow and Horrell brothers Tom and Sam were attacked by playful Apaches about twenty miles outside Las Cruces. Forty-eight-year-old Sam got his candle snuffed in the first volley of arrows and gunfire. A desperate Sallie Ann Horrell grabbed the dead man's revolver, hovered over her terrified children, and helped keep up a steady barrage of fire with her frantic brother-in-law Tom. The angry Native Americans finally gave up on scalping the whole party of white devils and eventually fled back into the harsh landscape they so adeptly and often used to their advantage anytime they went out on one of their raids.

Another version of the story has it that the Horrell clan couldn't get along with their New Mexican neighbors at all and the bad blood that grew up between the two factions resulted in several shootings, cattle theft on both sides, and even Horrell involvement in the Lincoln County War. Whatever the final account really might have been, the cantankerous Texans did eventually decide they'd had about all they ever wanted of New Mexico and beat a hasty path back to Lone Star heaven. Some say they were accompanied by a nagging band of back shooters who dogged their path almost all the way to the border.

Anyway, they all resettled around Lampasas and went back to ranching. 'Course along the return path from the gun smoke filled fiasco in New Mexico, they'd lost their entire herd and now found it necessary to completely rebuild from the bottom up. Lo and behold, people all over south central Texas started missing livestock, and charges of cow thievery got loosely tossed about.

The blood-soaked dustup between Pink Higgins and the remaining Horrells seems to have had its beginnings during the cow borrowing years just prior to the actual commencement of hostilities by the two angry packs of dogs. Most folks seem to think that the genesis of the whole shebang occurred on a January afternoon in 1873. Shortly after lunch that day Texas State

Chapter 5

Police Captain T.W. "Tom" Williams rode into Lampasas accompanied by seven other officers including one black gentleman.

The good captain and his cohorts had been summoned after Sheriff S.T. Denson tried to arrest a drunken amigo of the residual Horrells named Mark Short. Short's brother, Wash, helped him in the disagreement, and Sheriff Denson ended up on the ground with several bullet holes in his hide.

Captain Williams' orders, received directly from F.L. Britton, chief of the state police, included banning the use of firearms within the Lampasas town limits and seeing to it that those responsible for the shooting of Sheriff Denson spent some time in the local calaboose. And if they just by chance managed to kill a few troublesome Horrell types along the way, so much the better.

The good captain made the mistake of telling everyone he met on his trek into town just exactly what he intended to do to that bunch of "damned Horrels" when he found them. But he figured he'd settle their hash after he'd had one more for the road, and by the time he and his company arrived in town, most folks seem to agree that he'd been to the dipper a few times too many.

As the troop of state policeman reined up under a clump of live oaks in front of the Matador Saloon, Williams watched as a cowboy wearing a pistol turned and eased inside. Using what has been described as "proper caution," the lawman had half his men cover the outside of the building, left the black officer in charge of the horses, and proceeded inside with his remaining party.

What he couldn't have even remotely guessed was that behind the Matador's swinging doors a gathering comprised of Mart, Tom, and Merritt Horrell, their three brothers-in-law, the two Short brothers, and as many as ten other heavily armed cowboy type buddies lounged at the bar, played pool or poker, and generally enjoyed the classically rendered banjo and fiddle music available from the resident professor of background noise. Try to picture a classic 'B' western scene where every eye turns to the front of the saloon as the hated lawmen enter, spurs a jingling.

Williams didn't waste any time. He boldly moseyed over to the bar and ordered a drink. He knocked back his shot of Ol' Barn Burner and marched right up into the face of the armed cowboy he'd spotted out on the porch—a Horrell brother-in-law named Bill Bowen—and said something like, "I believe you're carrying a pistol, sir. I place you under arrest."

A contentious Mart Horrell is reported to have replied from the neighborhood of the billiards table, "Bill, you don't have to be arrested if you don't want to."

Well that really flung the fat in the fire, and wouldn't you just know, two different versions of what happened next ended up getting told by whatever partisan happened to be in charge of the story telling. One version claimed that Williams jumped on Bowen like a hungry mountain lion, and as the men fought over Bowen's pistol, any of the Horrells who weren't busy listening to the banjo music hopped behind a quickly overturned table—pistols a blazin'.

The second tale has it that as Mart Horrell let off his flume of buffalo gas, Williams drew his pistol and shot ol' Mart faster'n God could get there. After that invitation to dance everyone joined in on the fun, and a good time killing everything in sight was had by one and all.

When the gun smoke finally cleared, the score was Horrells 4, state police 0. Captain Williams and a fellow officer named Daniels died staring at their own reflections in the brass spittoons in front of the bar. Wesley Cherry, who evidently knew a bad deal when he saw it, headed for the safety of the street. Unfortunately someone dropped him just outside the doorway.

Chapter 5

Andrew Melville actually made it to the dusty street, but another "unknown gunman" drilled him about the time he hit the door of the Huling Hotel. He died an agonizing death in a bed at the Huling four weeks later. The three remaining policemen managed to get away relatively unscathed.

When he got word of the disaster in Lampasas, Adjutant General Britton decided that if he wanted them damned Horrells straightened out he'd have to do it himself. He fogged into town, gold braid and all, at the head of a company of state policeman and arrested Mart, who didn't manage to get out of Williams' line of fire quick enough, and two other men. Tom, Merritt, Bill Bowen, and everyone else who shot somebody, had conveniently managed to disappear like a Comanche war party headed for the plains. Britton dragged the bullet riddled Mart about halfway back to Austin, but decided to drop the wounded man off in Georgetown so he could recuperate from his wounds. The general made a serious mistake when he allowed Mart's wife, Artemisa, to stay on at the jail as the wounded prisoner's health care provider.

Artemisa did a hell of a nursing job on ol' Mart, and two months later she sent the family word that he had recovered enough to ride a horse. On May 2, 1873, the Horrell brothers led a squadron of heavily armed men right up to the door of the jail. While the gang stood guard with rifles, Bill Bowen stepped down from his horse, sledgehammer in hand, and knocked the flimsy gate off its hinges.

A sizable party of irate citizens from Georgetown tried to jerk a kink in the festivities, but when the firing became general and a local lawyer managed to get himself shot not once but twice, they all beat a hasty retreat back to the safety of home. Hell, no point getting killed over a stinking Horrell for Pete's sake!

Later that year Governor Ed Davis lost the election to Richard Coke after the Union army of occupation picked up and left the state. The state police force, heartily despised by one and all, was disbanded, and the Frontier Battalion of the Texas Rangers was organized in 1874 by Major John B. Jones.

The Horrell brothers got word from friends in Lampasas that if they ever wanted to get right with the law, the moment had arrived. They gave themselves over for trial, bonded out, and waited (this is sometimes referred to as the Jim Miller method). When a typical Texas style trial of the time finally got held in October 1876, a typical Texas style gathering of twelve good men and true never even bothered to leave the jury box when they voted for acquittal of the Horrells for killing the four roundly hated state policemen.

With their legal problems behind them, the Horrell boys took a spread out on Mesquite Creek and went to rebuilding their herds again, using the same old tried and true get 'em where you can method. They lived in relative harmony with the rest of the community during this period. But they also continued to get drunk in Lampasas' most popular watering holes and pretty much basked in the glory of the reputations their notoriety as men who'd killed policemen, broken out of jail, and fought the law, Indians, and damned near everyone else brought them.

Unfortunately the Horrell boys made a mistake they'd all live to regret. Family and associates started stealing cows from Pink Higgins, and what the thieving bastards didn't know was that the Pinker was a lot more ruthless and a sight more accomplished in the use of a rifle than any of them could have ever imagined.

By the time they'd managed their miracle in court, the Horrell clan had also gained considerable repute as men who would mishandle your stock given a dark night, or even a shady afternoon, and the chance. Ah yes, those carefree days as happy-go-lucky kids in New Mexico just having a good time with someone else's cows were gone forever—replaced by suspicious neighbors who didn't like it anytime one of the Horrell clan was spotted skulking around in the mesquite.

The man most vocal in the accusations department was none other than our good buddy and angry cow stuffer Pink Higgins. By this point Pink was twenty-five years old, tall, rugged as a stucco bathtub, and stronger than the case-hardened metal used in Colt's pistols. The life he'd led as a rancher and trail driver had honed his skills, and he was not a man to be trifled with. Worst of all, it tended to be beyond stupidity to let him catch you stealing his cows.

The reader shouldn't operate under the misconception that Lampasas was close on to as peaceful as the garden of Eden except for that fractious little Horrell-Higgins disagreement. No, my dear friends, plenty of other folks around town went for pistols and knives at the least provocation too. The diary of the knife and gun was vivid and bloody.

In 1875 William Bitnal bit the dust when Charles Keith shot the hell out of him. Keith got sentenced to jail for two years in Burnet but decided he could only stay around for a year and escaped with the ubiquitous Bill Bowen, well-known brother-in-law to the Horrell tribe. In November of that same year, a deputy sheriff named Douglass tried to arrest a disagreeable dentist. Dr. J.W. Hudson didn't like having his shorts jerked up around his Adam's apple, pulled a pistol, and the deputy killed the snot out of him.

Then in 1876 Wash Short's troublemaking brother Mark finally got arrested for the shooting of Sheriff Denson back in 1873. No record of his subsequent trial exists, but indications are that he probably got off like a good many others with the all-purpose plea of self-defense. Short didn't live very long after that though. Denson's son caught him in a saloon and blasted the tar out of him.

At about the same time the Short-Denson dustup worked itself out, a local lawyer named Hamilton got his feathers ruffled when Newton Cook called him a son-of-a-bitch. Hamilton pulled a derringer on the offending Mr. Cook and immediately tried to shoot off his own hand. The astonished Cook jerked his hog leg and chased Hamilton to every corner of the town square while Constable Elwood Bean trailed Hamilton, screaming and waving his gun. Must have been a kind of Keystone cowboys deal.

As all the fun with guns was popping up around town, the cattle thievery business continued and in some cases got blazingly blatant. Merritt Horrell stole a Pink Higgins yearling that almost ended up in a meat market owned by Horrell's brother-in-law. Higgins just happened to ride into Lampasas in the nick of time and spotted the animal tied to a tree in the town square. He took his property back and had Horrell arrested and proved in court, beyond any shadow of a doubt, the animal was his and that the thieving Merritt had no claim to it. Didn't matter a whit; the jury brought in a verdict of not guilty.

Pink put the word out for all the Horrells, their sizable extended family, and anyone else within earshot of a three-pound field piece that he wouldn't bother the law with such problems again. No bubba, he planned to settle any future cattle disputes with the business end of a Winchester model 1873 rifle.

Merritt, who must have had an IQ about half his boot size, let his success in the courts go to his head. He got so biggety that on January 20, 1877, he tried to use some more of Pink's cows to pay off a debt he owed a stock dealer named Alex Northington. Higgins got wind of the deal and once more rescued his animals. He left word for Horrell that if the thieving slug wanted to try and get them back they'd be easy to find in a local cattle-holding pen.

Merritt's available brain cells managed to recognize a threat when they heard one. He headed for the Matador Saloon and tried to lay low. Pink went home and nursed a rapidly growing hatred for the man he'd now caught stealing from him twice.

On Monday January 22 Higgins surprised the patrons of the Matador when he stepped inside from the icy cold, Winchester in hand. Things got real quiet real quick as the crowd sucked back and revealed a shivering Merritt Horrell standing near a stove in the back of the room trying to get warmed up.

In a voice as calm as a frozen pond Pink said something like, "Mr. Horrell, I think this should settle our cow business."

Then he snapped off a round that caught Horrell dead center, bounced him off a wall, and knocked him to the floor. But the wounded cow thief staggered to his feet and grabbed the shoulder of a friend to support his wobbling gait. If he thought Pink Higgins was finished he had another think coming. The Pinkster popped him again. This time Horrell couldn't muster the wherewithal to rise to the occasion, but just to make sure he'd done the job right, Higgins walked over to the fallen man and put two more in him just for good measure.

Higgins and some of his men jumped in the saddle and rode hell bent for the Horrell ranch out on Mesquite Creek. There existed no stated plan, but everyone pretty much agreed that rubout day had arrived for the Horrells and anyone who might want to help them. Somewhere along the way the angry bunch ran into Tom Horrell. A sizzling debate over what to do with him following his accidental capture was hot and feisty. The consensus seemed to be, "let's shoot him now 'cause if we don't we'll jest have to do it sometime later anyhow." But Pink's brothers-in-law Bill Wren and Bob Mitchell argued against the cold-blooded murder and pointed out that Tom carried no firearm with which to defend himself. Well the old code of the West got the best of Pink, and he reluctantly allowed his hated enemy to be released.

Company C of the Texas Rangers got called in, and although some of Pink's allies were arrested and thrown in the hoose-gow, they all ended up back out on the streets in pretty short order. Higgins remained free and did as he pleased. Word from that period indicates the rangers didn't make any seriously determined effort to find him because all he'd done was kill a rustlin' piece of scum so low he'd steal acorns from a blind sow and kick her for squealing.

Almost exactly two months after the Pinker whacked Merritt in the Matador, word got around that the two most prominent remaining Horrells were supposed to appear in Judge W.A. Blackburn's court. (Unfortunately history does not further enlighten us by recording why.) A party of Texas Rangers rode into town and surrounded the courthouse just in case the Higgins bunch decided to cause trouble.

Well, that ol' Pinkster is reported to have fooled them all again. He, Bill Wren, and a small group of their bubbas hid in the bushes along a creek about five miles out of town and waited for the Horrells to show themselves. The brothers stopped to water their horses and were immediately confronted with a blistering wall of gunfire from the opposite bank.

Tom fell from his horse during the first volley with a bullet in his hip. Mart got nicked in the neck, jumped from his animal, Winchester blazing, and charged the creek, blasting away with such red-eyed fury the Higgins party beat a hasty retreat—at least that's the way the story gets told even to this day. It does seem a bit odd, when you think about it, that a man of Higgins' hot-blooded, fire-forged audacity and friends just as courageous would run from a single man standing in the open roadway firing at a sizable number of those who had the cover of the trees. Makes your head hurt don't it?

Anyway, the wounded Horrells managed to make it to town and the rangers, led by a still bleeding Mart, hit the trail a running. After considerable sign reading, sleeping on the ground, and full bore detective work, they arrested one man, Bill Tinker. Both the Horrell brothers identified Tinker as being one of the shooters, but he promptly hit them with an ironclad alibi and got summarily released. Warrants for the arrest of Bill Wren floated around, but he went into hiding for a spell. When he finally came back to town, no one bothered him with anything like the pesky details of the now infamous *Battle Creek* shooting.

The rangers, under the command of a Captain Sparks, maintained a healthy presence in the area, and toward the end of April Higgins and Bob Mitchell gave themselves up. Both men were allowed bail in the rather hefty sum of $10,000 along with Judge Blackburn's heartfelt expectation of "better times in the future."

Well, Judge Blackburn, Captain Sparks, the editors of the *Lampasas Dispatch*, the local ladies aid society, the WCTU, and every citizen who would love to have seen peace prevail in the valley were in for a big surprise. On a dark and stormy June night, someone burglarized the courthouse and managed to selectively steal every piece of legal paper even remotely relating to the various Horrell-Higgins lawsuits awaiting resolution. A few days later a whole new Pecos promenade occurred that helped start a fresh and even bigger pile of court documents.

Having learned of the theft of records relating to their bond status, Higgins and Bob Mitchell decided to check in with the court and make sure everything was still kosher with the judge. On Thursday June 7 they strolled up to a position just outside town in the company of about a dozen heavily armed compadres. Pink, Bill Wren, Bob Mitchell, and Ben Terry proceeded into town and stumbled upon a festering nest of Horrells and their belligerent supporters. The Horrells spotted the Higgins bunch, grabbed their six-shooters, and started pouring lead in the general direction of the Star Hotel, Justo's Gun Shop, and the wagon yard at the corner of Second and Live Oak Streets. Wren tried to take cover behind a tree in the wagon yard near the Star Hotel. Mitchell ducked into the alley behind Justo's.

Pink and Ben Terry, who had been riding behind their friends, raced back to the outskirts of town for reinforcements. Wren gave up his tree and darted into the open street in an effort to get to Mitchell. A single shot caught him in the upper thigh and almost knocked him off his feet as he stumbled to his friend's side. Mitchell helped Wren into the back door of a building that housed the Yates and Brown Store on the ground floor. They struggled to the second level and sought safety in the law offices of Judge J.A. Abney. Mitchell's brother, Frank—who had never had any part in the disagreement prior to that day—in town on business at Yates and Brown, saw Bob being attacked and although unarmed also made it to the second floor with the Higgins followers.

Wren handed him a gun. Frank slipped back downstairs and stepped out the front door of Yates and Brown's just in time to spot Mart Horrell and Jim Buck Miller coming out the side door of Fulton and Townsen's Store across Third Street. Frank popped Jim Buck dead center, and all the Horrell guns turned on him at the same time. A Winchester slug caught him in the chest and drove him back inside Yates and Brown's where he fell behind the counter and died. Mart Horrell would later claim credit for the killing of a universally well-liked citizen who happened to be in the wrong place at the wrong time.

Mart dragged the wounded Jim Buck Miller—who died a day later—down an alley to a rock building that was still under construction. When Pink Higgins came crashing back into town at the head of his backers, the entire Horrell bunch had holed up behind the newly erected rock walls and couldn't, according to an overheated newspaper account, have been driven out "by a regiment of men."

The fighting and sniping went on for hours and at times proceeded with what was described as "great ferocity." Higgins recognized that the struggle probably wasn't about to go anywhere and when approached by concerned Lampasas business leaders agreed to sheath his rifle and ride out of town. The Horrells allowed themselves to be arrested and placed into protective custody. Once it got dark they were released, probably by way of some kind of previously worked out deal with local lawmen, and headed for their own homes.

According to Bill O'Neal in his excellent little book *A Half Century of Violence in Texas—The Bloody Legacy of Pink Higgins,* the *Lampasas Leader* reported that afterwards, "Turmoil and excitement prevailed all over the country," and that "people were expecting every day to hear of a clash between warring factions." Hell, if people started shooting each other in downtown Dallas or Fort Worth today you can bet "turmoil and excitement would prevail" now too.

Well suffice it to say that the town's leadership was fit to be tied over a two-hour shooting that resulted in a couple of extremely dead men and at least one more seriously wounded. Just nothing like a little gunfire and dying on a town's busiest streets to get the chamber of commerce types excited. Lampasas had, since its earliest settlement, drawn those who believed the local waters of Sulphur Creek were of great medicinal benefit. The town could justifiably look back to its original establishment as having derived from this a steady string of visitors seeking the cleansing and healthful waters of Lampasas' own natural moneymaker. Dry goods, grocery stores, drug stores, and to some degree local saloons and dance halls all benefited from the tourist trade. The men who owned those businesses realized that something had to be done, and damned quick, to put an end to total warfare in their streets.

To that end the town's suspender poppers got Sheriff Albertus Sweet to petition Major John B. Jones for some much-needed heavy artillery relief. Jones, who commanded the Frontier Battalion of the Texas Rangers, assembled a detail of fifteen men and arrived in Lampasas about a week after the by-now infamous Horrell-Higgins shootout. The rangers helped the sheriff arrest everyone in sight who even looked like he might be about to do something wrong. Problem was that none of the arrests involved any of the Horrells, Pink Higgins, or the followers of either of them.

A simple reason existed for the rangers' inability to put those responsible for the shootings and killings under lock and key: The angriest and most violent had all left the country or gone into deep hiding. But when the Horrells finally started trickling back into the area about a month later, Major Jones launched negotiations with both sides to bring an end to the feuding. While those talks proceeded, an anonymous killer busted a cap on a Higgins partisan named Carson Graham. With Graham's journey to that great cattle drive in the sky, Major Jones redoubled his efforts to put an end to the feud.

When his investigations of the murder turned up nothing but fingers pointing in the Horrell clan's direction, he decided to get serious with the ornery bunch. He ordered Ranger Sergeant N.O. Reynolds and seven privates to find the entire Horrell crew and put them all under arrest.

With the help of Bill Wren and Bob or Alonzo Mitchell, Sergeant Reynolds and his men located the Horrell stronghold, waited until early in the morning when everyone was sound asleep, crept inside, leveled guns on one and all, and then woke them up. A little struggling and a lot of mean mouthing ensued, but Reynolds made it clear that the rangers had them covered and that if the outlaw family didn't give it up he would be forced to have his men open fire and probably wipe out the entire tribe at the same time. After having received Reynolds' word that he would see to their safety, Mart Horrell decided it best for friends and family to lay down their weapons and go in peaceably.

The bottom line outcome of all this arresting and stuff was that Major Jones managed to negotiate a document of settlement from each of the warring parties. The Texas Ranger, a classically educated former Confederate army officer from South Carolina, put a high price on appearances. His skillfully worded agreements elicited promises from all the members of both parties to lay down their guns and refrain from future insulting behavior that could lead to any further fighting. Everyone involved eventually signed off on the deal, and the *Lampasas Dispatch* boldly and, you have to admit, somewhat hopefully announced:

> *PEACE RESTORED IN LAMPASAS!*
> *THE HIGGINS AND HORRELL PARTIES*
> *HAVE LAID DOWN THEIR ARMS!*

But peace is pretty much the same everywhere. It's no better than the people who put their names to it. The Horrells might not have done any more fighting with Pink Higgins and his friends, but hell, everyone knew they couldn't stay out of trouble for long, and like a self-fulfilling prophecy, they didn't.

Little more than six months after they swore to make nice, in May 1878, a gang of cutthroats robbed a Bosque County storekeeper named J.F. Vaughn of $3,000 and decided it would be a good idea not to leave anyone around to testify against them. He died in a storm of gunfire, but several witnesses stumbled on the robbery and sent the thieves into the night on their own wave of hot lead. Investigators tracked a wounded horse from the scene of the murder to the corral of a man named Bill Crabtree. Crabtree had for years been one of the Horrells' best bubbas. But when confronted with the possibility of a little cow pasture justice for the well-liked Mr. Vaughn's untimely passing, brother Crabtree sang like the proverbial bird with an almost religious zeal that impressed all those who heard it. He implicated everyone in the Vaughn murder from the Horrell brothers to Davy Crockett.

A forward thinking judge from Meridian, in Bosque County, by the name of Childress ordered Mart and Tom Horrell jailed forthwith. On September 8, 1878, lawdogs brought the brothers to heel and dragged them back to the judge's court for a hearing. Childress didn't particularly like what he heard in his hearing and ordered them held for trial. Crabtree tried to slink out of town. But just as he reached Meridian's city limits, a mysterious and unidentifiable gunman blasted Crabtree from his saddle and left him to die under a tree near the manure littered dirt roadway.

Judge Blackburn tried to get the Horrell boys returned to Lampasas by way of extradition, but Childress wouldn't give them up. He sent Blackburn a letter in which he described feelings in Meridian as running so hot that he could not vouch for their safety if released from custody. Unfortunately for the Horrells, Judge Childress' faith in the strength and safety of the local jail was just a shade misplaced.

After almost four months sitting in a cell picking at whatever they could find to pick at, on December 15, 1878, someone lured Meridian's sheriff away from his jail with a story that his mother had fallen down dead and the hogs were after her. He'd barely gotten out of sight when a hundred masked vigilantes bluffed their way inside the lockup by someone announcing himself as "Deputy Whitworth."

Getting inside the jail was one matter, getting the prisoners out was a whole different deal. The jailers refused to open the cellblock, and the mob was somewhat frustrated for a bit. But then one of the merrymakers brought up a can of kerosene and threatened to turn their local pokey into a smoldering pile of charcoal briquettes. Well the keys came out pretty quick after that, and the crowd surged past the initial set of bars to the holding cells where the Horrells were located.

This turned out to be one of those lynchings where you didn't need a rope. Everyone with a gun locked, loaded, took aim, and blasted the hell out of the Horrell of their choice. The story goes that Tom cowered in a corner and tried to keep from getting hit by the hail of bullets, but Mart stood up and took it the same way he did in that little dustup out on Battle Branch.

Some of the shooters even testified that a frothing-at-the-mouth Mart grabbed the bars of his cell, rattled them like an enraged animal, and roundly cursed the mob even after he'd been plugged a number of times. Although it has never been proven, there were those who believed that Pink Higgins and Bob Mitchell acted as members of the Meridian rabble and in some stories led the mob.

But the hard feelings and death still hadn't managed to run their course. Sam Horrell, the only one of the entire troublesome family to survive, mainly because he seems to have taken little or no part in any of the worst of their activities, decided that rather than go the way of all his brothers he'd get the hell out of Dodge—or Lampasas as it were. He packed his family up (some believe with more than a little encouragement from ole Pink or his friends), headed for California, and lived to the extremely ripe old age of ninety-nine when he passed away in his sleep in 1936.

Folks who rode with the Horrells and thought the violence was finally over had more than a few surprises coming. About nine months after the good citizens of Meridian—if that's what they actually were—punched the brothers' tickets for the hereafter, a bunch of men rode up to the Mesquite Creek home of James Collier. Collier, a close personal friend of the formerly living Mart Horrell, assured his wife that everything would be fine and agreed to leave with the nightriders. She watched from their porch as he accompanied them into the inky darkness. The next day his body was found hanging from a tree limb not far from his home. A crudely scribbled sign hanging around the dead man's skinny shoulders warned that all "THEAVES AND MURDURES—WIL BE SERVED—THE SAME—WAY."

A few days later a group of unidentified riders approached the Vanwinkle brothers' camp out on Little Lucy Creek, north of town. A man who claimed to be the sheriff of some place or another ordered Bill Vanwinkle to come along with them. About half an hour after he agreed to go with the "sheriff," his brothers Tom and Jesse heard gunfire. The next morning they found poor ol' Bill's perforated body a short distance from where he'd been abducted.

Things leveled out for about three months. Then in August a midnight posse lit up the countryside again when they hemmed the Kinchelo brothers up in their stepfather's home. The vigilantes demanded that the men come outside, and when both made a run for it, the volley killed William in the front yard and wounded his brother Gus, who still managed to escape.

None of the shooters in any of these three anonymous killings were ever identified, arrested, or brought to the bar of justice. Most folks didn't really care if they ever were. The dead men all sported reputations as cattle and horse thieves or friends of the Horrells or both. Such vocations and associations tended to lead any thinking person to acknowledge that the Higgins party most probably helped them into the hereafter. But you could have bet the ranch and all your cows that damned few had nerve enough to say it out loud or even begin to act like they were offended by what went on. It wouldn't have been healthy by a wagonload.

For the next thirty-three years, Pink Higgins' life cruised along with nothing like the kind of upheaval that marked his open warfare with the Horrell clan. Oh, there were a few little deeper than average ruts in the wagon road of his passing years. He and his first wife divorced. So much time invested riding the trails between Lampasas and the Kansas railheads took a heavy toll on their relationship. Such that when he learned of her infidelity with a new arrival in the area named Dunk Harris, he didn't even bother to kill the man.

About a year after his break-up with Betty was finalized on June 8, 1883, he married fifteen-year-old Lena Sweet. They eventually parented six children and, as trail driving declined with the passage of time, Pink and his new wife opened a combination meat market/saloon in Lampasas. But the business burned to the ground, and he had some difficulty collecting debts that amounted to thousands of dollars lost because his records of extended credit were consumed in the blaze.

In 1885 he entered into a horse buying deal with some Mexican traders in Ciudad Acuna across the Rio Grande from Del Rio. He paid the very pleasant horse-trading señors a dollar each in up-front money for 125 head of stock. Pink and three of his help crossed the river to pick up his property on the appointed day only to discover that no horse herd existed.

The Mexican traders thought it downright humorous that a silly gringo on their side of the border would have nerve enough to demand his money back. The man who took the down payment even had the brass to claim he'd never seen Señor Pink Higgins before and laughed right in the Texan's face.

Well, Pink eyeballed the careless talking caballero a moment, then said something like, "And you won't ever see me again," as he whipped out his Winchester and pumped the stupid goober's hide full of lead.

The angry Texan and his crew beat a hasty retreat toward the river chased by a storm of Mexican gunfire. One of his men fell dead and another was badly wounded before they reached the Rio Grande. The blocked international bridge forced them off their animals and into a running gun battle from hiding spots along the riverbank. An uninjured drover made it into the water and urged Pink to swim across with him. Pink refused to leave his wounded employee and forced his companions to stay and fight. Later in life he was quoted as saying that bullets fell around them "like hail stones."

By the time darkness came and they managed to get safely across the river, the three living Americanos had managed to put lead in several more of their tormentors. An older and wiser Higgins told friends he "fought harder and under less favorable circumstances that day" than he'd ever confronted before in his entire life. Given his toe-to-toe encounters with Comanches, thieves, and gunfighters, Pink managed to say a mouthful about his Mexican opponents of that bloody afternoon.

Confusion over ownership of a single animal put Higgins in prison for almost two years beginning in February of 1892. He traded a horse for a cow that he then tried to sell to a Lampasas meat market. When the beast's true brand was revealed under a patch of overgrown hair (animals such as these were referred to as "wild stags"), its owner claimed it as stolen. A jury of folks less than favorable to old gunfighters and cattle thieves convicted Pink of the theft and sentenced him to two years in the Rusk branch of the Texas State Penitentiary—an astonishingly ironic development when you consider his efforts in the past and his lifelong personal feelings about cow thieves.

Although he was well behaved and eligible for parole after serving half his sentence, prison officials kept him incarcerated for three quarters of the total prison term laid on him by the jury. By the time he was returned to freedom in the Lampasas area, the combination of time served and feelings of claustrophobia overcame him. He needed more in the way of wide-open spaces. In 1899 he left Lampasas to establish a home in Kent County on a spread near Catfish Creek—a little stream today called the White River—about seventy miles east and a bit south of Lubbock.

Shortly after arrival in his new digs, Pink took a position as a cattle detective or range rider for the huge Spurs ranch. Thieves left the area in droves when they heard that the Spurs had hired Higgins to put an end to their problems with missing cattle. Didn't take long for ranch management to be so pleased they could almost hug themselves over the results of their decision to put the old cow finder on the payroll.

But he soon ran into problems with another Spurs stock detective named Billy Standifer. Standifer also had lived in Lampasas at one time. His father once owned a local mercantile, and his family claimed a certain degree of past friendship with the Horrells. This and a variety of other reasons crop up when grounds are sought for the hard feelings between the two men. But in addition to all that, Pink felt that his counterpart was probably personally responsible for some of the stock disappearances, and when a building on Higgins' Catfish Creek property burned, he suspected Billy Standifer of the arson.

As tensions between the men grew, Spurs manager Fred Horsburg tried to separate the two growling dogs by showing Standifer the gate first and then telling Pink he had to be off Spurs property within a month. Indications are that Higgins had every intention of vacating the little house provided him by ranch management. But before he could pack up and get out, Standifer was spotted prowling around the area, and Pink indicated to friends and family that nothing good could come of it.

On Wednesday October 1, 1902, Standifer and Higgins ran into each other a short distance from Pink's little company house. The rifle duel that followed only lasted a few seconds. Both men jumped from their horses, and the gunfire commenced apace. Billy fired first and managed to hit Pink's mount. As his dying horse, Sandy, headed back home for the corral, Higgins dropped to one knee, took careful aim, and drilled his assailant with a slug that sliced through his upper arm and lodged in his chest. Standifer died within a few seconds of being hit.

When Pink reported to Sheriff N.N. Rogers that he thought maybe he'd killed Standifer, he must have been pleased beyond words when the sheriff replied, "Well, if you're not sure, maybe you should go back and finish him off."

In what can only be described as a triumph of politics, Horsburg rehired Higgins as a stock detective. Why not? Standifer was dead and therefore no longer a problem to be worried about. And when Sheriff B.F. Roy took over from N.N. Rogers, he went a step further by appointing Pink deputy sheriff of Kent County. All for killing a man who had, only a short time earlier, enjoyed the love and respect of neighbors and employers.

From that point until his own passing, things went pretty well for Pink. He enjoyed his cattle detective and law enforcement work, developed his Catfish Creek ranch, and in 1904 when he returned to Lampasas to take care of some family business, he benefited from the respectful treatment usually accorded those considered well-known pioneers.

A few years prior to his death, a woman named Jones asked Higgins if he really had killed fourteen men. He told her that it got to a point for a while around Lampasas that anytime a corpse popped up near town everybody said, "Pink Higgins did it." But he went on to point out, "I didn't kill all them men, but then again I got some that wasn't on the bill, so I guess it about evens up."

On December 18, 1913, while stoking the coals in the fireplace of his Catfish Creek ranch, John Calhoun Pinckney "Pink" Higgins clutched his chest and dropped dead on the stones of his own hearth. He was sixty-two years old.

Anyone operating under the misconception that the passing of Pink Higgins would result in peace upon the land was in for a rude shock. A few years prior to ol' Pink's exit from this life, a man named Si Bostick was tried and acquitted for an act of cattle theft of which he was most likely guilty. This single event laid the groundwork for more shootings, more killings, more convictions, and the involvement of such famed Texans as the redoubtable ranger legend Frank Hamer. But amigos, as the old campfire bull feather artists liked to say, that's a whole 'nother story. And if you're really interested, go out and buy yourself a copy of Bill O'Neal's terrific book on Pink and the eventual outcome of it all. Suffice it to say that in a manner much like that seen in the great blood feuds that have destroyed countries in Europe, the Horrell-Higgins affair lasted until just about everyone who gave a damn was extremely dead and in the ground.

Pink Higgins managed to live his life in such a manner as to be the absolute paradigm of the "good" killer described in the opening pages of the previous chapter on Jim Miller. He did not hide behind a rock and slaughter his prey by shooting them in the back. There exists no evidence that he ever killed an enemy from the cover of a nice dark tree line, and no one ever accused him of having been paid for the brutal death of another human being just because someone with money wanted the poor slub dead. No, the Pinkster's victims, so far as he was concerned (and so far as can be determined) deserved exactly what they got. They were stock stealing sons-of-bitches and didn't need to be breathing the same air as "good folks." Blessed be the word of the avenger carrying a Winchester model '73.

Chapter 6

No White Man Can Arrest Me, or, You Can't Arrest Me For Nothing!

Gregorio Cortez Lira

Even recent history has its own versions of the old saw that one man's hero is often another man's villain. All too often these differences of opinion are based exclusively on what people claim they saw or knew about the person in question. Minimally skilled lawyers have long known that eyewitness identification or descriptions of events are some of the least reliable ways of getting to the bottom of any occurrence. Today hours and hours of actual classroom time are spent in most law schools training our up-and-coming young barristers on how to evaluate such evidentiary possibilities. Testimony from the person who "was there and saw it all" is still viewed as some of the most powerful that can be presented in a courtroom. This in spite of the fact that most professional law enforcement types will freely admit it is usually some of the least reliable information that can be placed before a jury for consideration. The more witnesses you have the less reliable their testimony usually is. Policemen know this very singular and telling fact because a dozen people who view the same event at the same time will inexplicably come away with a totally different impression of what often occurred within a few feet of their faces.

Recently one of the three major television networks devoted an entire hour's worth of prime time to an examination of this exact problem. They conducted an old and familiar college speech teacher's trick-experiment on a new audience. Forty graduate level law students sat in an amphitheater and watched as an intruder entered the room, snatched the instructor's purse from her desk, and ran.

A skilled investigator then questioned each member of the group as a witness to the crime. The physical description of the thief and exactly what had occurred flopped all over the map like a gaffed tuna. The one member of the group who managed to get closer to the purse-snatcher than anyone else swore the thief wore a nonexistent baseball cap. When shown a videotape of the actual event exactly as it occurred, this witness concluded, independent of all existing proof to the contrary, that it obviously wasn't the man he'd seen.

Most elementary school children have played an old game called "gossip." The teacher whispers a message into the ear of a student at the front of the room and it is in turn passed behind the hand to every other child until it has made its snakelike circuit around the room. By the time the message arrives at the last person to receive it the meaning has usually changed so much as to be totally unrecognizable. "Gossip" and let's play eyewitness all too often lead to the same result—poor or questionable information. People tend to see and hear exactly what they want and then interpret it in ways that defy the imagination of the best fiction writers on the planet.

Perhaps no other story of Texas gunfire and death from the distant past of our shared history works to illustrate this hypothesis half as well as the saga of Gregorio Cortez. His brush with frontier justice owes its total existence to off-the-mark eyewitnesses, botched language interpretation, and out-right goofy meanderings by people given to believing anything anyone wanted to add to the dramatic events of a single summer in his life.

Born to Roman Cortez Garza and Rosalia Lira Cortina near Matamoros, Tamaulipas Mexico on June 22, 1875, his family migrated to Manor, Texas (near Austin) in 1887. Typical of the time, the young Gregorio worked as an itinerant farm laborer. Two years after his family's arrival in *el norte*, he and his brother Romaldo traveled to Karnes, Gonzales, and other surrounding counties where they took employment as vaqueros or worked in the fields. This transient quality to his life-style would later be used to explain his extensive knowledge of the geography of the area.

On February 20, 1890, at the tender age of fifteen, he married Leonor Diaz. This union resulted in four children. Mariana made her entry on the scene in 1891 when her father had barely turned sixteen. Nine years after his first daughter's birth, Gregorio—by now twenty-five years old and the father of four children—and his brother Romaldo decided to try working for themselves instead of other people. They rented a piece of land about ten miles from Kennedy in Karnes County from a man named Thulemeyer, built homes within a mile of each other, and settled in for the life of working farmers. By midsummer of the following year they had a corn crop envied by everyone in the area.

The Cortez brothers enjoyed the reputation among their neighbors as being hard working, sober, well liked, and not given to causing trouble. But they suffered from a problem well known to folk of their ancestral background. They were Mexicans, and everyone who wasn't a Mexican knew that you just couldn't trust those people. In fact the Anglo mind of the time tended to operate under some powerful and closely held beliefs when it came to their brothers from south of the border.

Common knowledge, for instance, indicated that most Mexicans were malicious, gutless, untrustworthy thieves who took special pleasure in stealing livestock, stabbing white Texans in the back, and generally living the lives of those who hadn't advanced quite far enough along the evolutionary scale. Such beliefs guaranteed that men like John Wesley Hardin and Jim Miller could arbitrarily murder Mexican citizens at a rate that made it impossible to keep an accurate count of them.

This nineteenth-century method of what we would today refer to as racial profiling was so pervasive that people of Mexican decent believed it influenced their treatment at the hands of Texas's most famous law enforcement body—the Texas Rangers. Unjustifiable arrests and killings often resulted in stories told all along the border to illustrate just how dangerous it was to be caught RWM—riding or walking while Mexican.

One of the most famous of these tales demonstrated beyond any doubt just how bad Mexican citizens felt their status in the eyes of the law really was. Seems, as the story was told, some rangers set out to catch a Mexican stock thief and stayed on his trail until they ran into a group of field hands on their way home from a hard day's work. The rangers, frustrated by their inability to catch the real thief, killed as many of the laborers as they could and reported back to their superiors that they were attacked by a large number of armed Mexican desperados. In spite of being grossly outnumbered, the courageous lawmen still managed to successfully eradicate at least a dozen of the villains in self-defense and chase the rest back across the Rio Grande into Mexico. Keep in mind that this yarn was labeled *apocryphal* from the very beginning, but like most such stories it probably contained more than a melon-sized kernel of truth. It was an expedition such as the one just described that would eventually lead to the legendary status later accorded corn farmer Gregorio Cortez Lira.

On or about June 9, 1901, third-term Karnes County sheriff W.T. (Brack) Morris got word from the Atascosa County sheriff that he should keep a wary eye peeled for a horse thief who had made off with a sorrel mare. The thief was described as being Mexican, medium sized, and wearing a red, broad-brimmed Mexican hat. Now you don't really have to have a doctorate in thermonuclear science to be able to figure out that what Sheriff Morris got was an open invitation to go out and grab just about any Mexican available and drag him in for stock theft. If the aforementioned arrestee resisted, well a dead Mexican thief was just as good as a live one.

Morris deserves at least a little credit for not simply walking outside the door of his official county sheriff's office and randomly shooting people in the street. He did make a half-hearted effort at some actual detective work by trailing a single horse from the Karnes County line almost to Kenedy. And on the morning of June 12, 1901, he started a round of questioning that involved all Mexican citizens in his jurisdiction who had recently acquired new animals, especially sorrels.

As he made his way from one *casa* to the next the sheriff was accompanied by two of his deputies, John Trimmell and a man named Boone Choate who acted as his interpreter. Hard to believe, but the Karnes County sheriff could speak just about enough Spanish to order a *cerveza* and it would prove to be his total undoing. Perhaps worse than Sheriff Morris' linguistic shortcomings were those of his supposed interpreter, Deputy Choate. The man had just enough knowledge to make him dangerous—as it turned out, very dangerous.

Chapter 6

No one reading this account should be operating under the misconception that the sheriff and his deputies rode around the countryside on their high-spirited palominos armed to the teeth and looking for a fight. Morris and his rustler hunters traveled in the sheriff's surrey, and of the three men only the sheriff and Deputy Trimmell remembered to bring a gun of some kind. More importantly, as evidence of their probable intentions that afternoon, none of the three men had bothered to swear out a warrant for anyone's arrest that day.

Since a good lawman was considered one who didn't beat the refried beans out of any Mexican he took the time to put under arrest, the sheriff was considered relatively friendly to most of the peons in the area. He was a former ranger and had managed to reach the rank of sergeant before being elected to the office of sheriff three times. Locals considered him fast and accurate with a handgun, and he was known to have used deadly force on numerous occasions. He was not a man to be taken lightly.

At some point during their round of investigating, the sheriff and his men developed information, through a Señor Andrés Villarreal, that led them to pay an official visit on Gregorio Cortez. Seems Villarreal had recently acquired a sorrel mare by way of a trade with the young farmer. The sheriff's poor methods of information gathering and inability to understand those he questioned in the case went downhill the minute he failed to have Boone Choate pursue his inquiries on the previous ownership of the mare in question. If he had done so, the men would have easily discovered that Villarreal possessed an intimate knowledge of the animal's original source and of Gregorio Cortez's indisputable legal ownership of the beast.

There is some reason to believe that Sheriff Morris took his deadly step in Cortez's direction because Gregorio and his brothers Tomas and Romaldo and their father had at one time or another been suspected of being involved in previous acts of stock theft. In fact charges were brought against Romaldo in 1887 but were eventually dropped. Tomas got a pardon from Governor Lawrence Ross for similar charges and then ended up being sentenced to five years in the pen for the same kind of offense in 1900.

Well, for whatever reason, Sheriff Morris decided to take a little ride over to the Cortez place and just check everything out to make sure it was all on the up and up—typical policeman thinking of any era since the beginning of time. The three lawmen bounced over to a spot about half a mile from the Cortez home and Trimmell got out of the surrey to do a little Sherlock Holmes stuff around a set of cattle pens located there. Choate would later swear that Morris left Trimmell in that strategic spot to cut off any attempt at escape the desperate Gregorio might make when confronted with arrest. Counter testimony at the trial would later establish this as a particularly useless tactic since the entire half mile between the pens and the house was covered with thick, almost impenetrable brush.

As Morris and Choate rode up to the house, what they saw was a rustic dwelling set in the middle of a clearing that had been hacked out of a mesquite thicket. Morris reined his horse to a stop at a gate in the fence about sixty feet from the front door. Lying on the floor of his covered porch, Gregorio had reclined with his head in his wife Leonor's lap for an afternoon siesta. Brother Romaldo relaxed on the steps, and as the lawman's surrey stopped, Gregorio sat up, slid his pistol from the front of his pants to a position in the small of his back, and told his brother to go find out what the gringos wanted.

Romaldo strolled over to the gate, and from that point on everything went to hell like a runaway stagecoach with no brakes. Choate asked for Gregorio Cortez. Romaldo turned back as though to retake his place on the steps and said to his brother as he walked, *"Te quieren."* A literal translation of the phrase would be "you are wanted" which is a common way in Spanish to say, "They want to talk to you." But that's not what Boone Choate heard. To his poorly trained interpreter's ear, what Romaldo meant was that the Cortez brothers both already knew that Gregorio was a wanted man. His mistake could not have resulted in deadlier consequences.

Later, all those present would testify that Gregorio rose, met his brother about halfway to the gate, and both moved to positions directly behind the fence and facing the two lawmen. Romaldo leaned against a post, and Gregorio stopped a few steps away as though he suspected something wayward was about to happen.

Choate continued the questioning in Spanish and asked if the Mexican farmer had recently traded a sorrel *horse* to Andrés Villarreal. The reply was "no." And as far as Gregorio Cortez was concerned it was the unvarnished truth. Cortez had traded a sorrel *mare,* and the distinction was critical to the conversation at hand—a distinction of which both Choate and Morris should have been acutely aware. The total breakdown in communications on this particular subject was probably due in large part to Deputy Choate's unreliable understanding of Spanish and the fact that he very likely couldn't come up with the word for mare (*yegua*) and instead used *caballo*—which means male horse.

As soon as the word "no" passed Cortez's lips, Morris, who already had testimony from Villarreal concerning the trade, climbed down from his surrey, pushed through the gate, and told Choate to inform the brothers that they were about to be handcuffed and arrested. He was said to be about five steps away and to the right of the two men when Choate's interpretation of their immediate incarceration hit the Cortez boys.

At that point the deputy's poor ability as an interpreter completely failed everyone involved in the unfolding scene. Gregorio said something that Boone conveyed to the sheriff that he thought sounded like, "No white man can arrest me." When confronted with the gross error of his mistake on the witness stand at the Cortez trial, he changed his testimony at least twice and still didn't get it right. In all likelihood what Gregorio actually said was, "You can't arrest me for nothing." Morris heard, "No white man can arrest me." For the frontier sheriff it was about the equivalent of a verbal slap in the face.

A variety of stories about what happened next came from Choate, Romaldo, Gregorio, his wife Leonor, and some of Cortez Lira's children who witnessed the affair. But of all the interpretations of the shooting (read less than dependable eyewitness accounts here), what follows is probably as accurate an explanation as can be had.

As far as County Sheriff Morris could tell, neither of the Mexicans were armed. He probably pulled his pistol with the intent of shooting Gregorio because the smart aleck Mexican had, as nearly as he could ascertain, just refused to be arrested and on top of that, according to Boone Choate, had done it in a fairly insulting manner.

Romaldo, in an effort to protect a brother he believed to be unarmed, saw the sheriff's pistol come out, launched himself off his fence post, and ran toward Morris, who fired a shot that struck the man in the mouth, exited though his cheek, and lodged in his shoulder. When he turned back to the original object of his intentions, Morris was stunned to discover his potential prisoner raising his own pistol and preparing to shoot.

Both men fired within a split-second of each other. The Morris shot went wild, but Gregorio's found its mark and almost knocked the sheriff to his knees. The wounded lawman managed to recover and thumbed off two or three more rounds.

Chapter 6

All of them hit various mesquite bushes, rocks, or fence posts. Cortez steadied up, took careful aim, and his second shot punched another monstrous hole in the sheriff and sent him staggering toward the gate and the possible safety of his surrey. Unfortunately he collapsed from shock and loss of blood before he got more than a few steps. Gregorio then strolled over to the fallen man and shot him again as he lay sprawled out on the ground.

As soon as the generalized gunfire commenced, Boone Choate started running. He hit the mesquite thickets and headed for the cattle pens where he and Sheriff Morris had left Deputy Trimmell. By the time those two brave men made it back to town, stories flew thick and fast that a whole gang of red-eyed, kill-crazed Mexicans had attacked the lawmen and murdered the hell out of poor ol' Sheriff Morris.

But if either or both of the yellow-bellied deputies had bothered to return to the scene of the crime before hotfooting it back to safety, they would have found that the entire Cortez family had abandoned their home and that Sheriff Morris was still alive but slowly bleeding to death from his wounds. The wounded lawdog even managed to stand and stagger some two hundred yards into the surrounding brush where he died before anyone could find him.

Within minutes of the shooting, Cortez and his badly wounded brother mounted horses and headed into the thick brush, traveling in a more or less straight line from his farm to Kenedy, ten miles away. He intended to slip into town after dark and get whatever medical help he could for Romaldo. But the difficult ride proved almost impossible. His delirious brother ranted, raved, and kept passing out and falling from his horse. About five miles from his house, Gregorio was forced to stop, lay his brother under a tree to rest, and wait till the situation got at least a little better.

His wife and family had left the scene of the crime in a wagon at the same time as the fugitive brothers. Leonor and the children were to take refuge with friends who lived just outside Kenedy. They barely got away from the house when the leading edge of the first posse arrived. Gregorio had instructed his daughter Mariana to tell anyone they met on the road that they lived on a ranch near town and were on the way home. Although stopped several times that day, not one man among the searchers doubted the word of his wife and children, and they went on their way virtually unmolested.

Meanwhile, Gregorio and Romaldo stayed hidden under their tree from early in the afternoon of the twelfth until it got dark. During the entire time, the ever-growing posse, or posses, thrashed through the brush all around them but failed to discover the desperados. They even failed to find poor dead Sheriff Morris, who had stumbled into the mesquite thickets and floated off to that great jailhouse in the sky less than two hundred yards from the house. The excuse given for this gross oversight was that the posse wasn't looking for two men or one wounded man. Oh no, they were valiantly searching for a whole band of Mexican outlaws collectively known as the Cortez Gang that they were absolutely certain had kidnapped Sheriff Morris and carried him away to Mexico. Now why Mexicans would abduct a Texas sheriff and spirit him off to unknowable parts south of the border was a question that didn't seem to need an answer. Hell, the searchers just assumed the truth of the outlandish tale and went storming into the brush like crazed longhorns.

Under cover of darkness and with a staggering amount of difficulty, Gregorio finally managed to get his wounded brother to the home of friends in Kenedy at about one o'clock in the morning. Romaldo's condition made it impossible for him to stay on a horse during the ordeal. Even though Gregorio sat behind him and tried to hold his brother upright, the delirious man kept falling off and in the end had to be carried most of the remaining five miles.

As soon as his mouth-shot brother was delivered into the hands of friends and family, infamous gang leader and murderer Gregorio Cortez slipped into the black of night and disappeared like a wisp of fog. Although he had two horses hidden nearby, the Mexican outlaw headed out on foot, and instead of going south as the posse would have expected, he struck out in the opposite direction. He planned to take refuge with acquaintances in Gonzales County and eventually head for Austin and Manor where he could safely hole up with his many relatives in the area. From Manor, obscurity in the north was a given. Clearly his plan worked; on June 13 the *San Antonio Express* confidently trumpeted, "The trail of the Mexican leads toward the Rio Grande."

The trip from Kenedy to Ottine in Gonzales County would be about sixty-five miles if you could manage to do it as the crow flies. But Gregorio didn't have that luxury and was forced to zigzag his way along the rough route by staying away from the main thoroughfares. Altogether it has been estimated that he covered approximately eighty miles in forty hours! He did it wearing a pair of low cut, pointy-toed, badly made leather shoes.

Many believe that the most dangerous portion of his dash for freedom occurred early on the morning of June 13 when he stopped in Runge for breakfast. He had no way of knowing that the little town, about eight miles north of Kenedy, was where the bullet-riddled recently departed Sheriff W.T. "Brack" Morris made his home or that the entire bereaved village planned to attend the dead lawman's funeral later that afternoon. Altogether Gregorio's steaming plate of *huevos rancheros* that morning might well have been one of the most risky meals he ever took the time to eat. There's every indication that if the citizens of Runge had recognized and caught the fugitive that morning, the expense of a trial could have been completely avoided.

With a belly full of victuals under his belt, Cortez Lira hit the deck running and in an amazing thirty-four hours managed to make it to Belmont, a town about fifty-five miles from Kenedy. He stopped at a friend's house to eat again then set out for the Schnabel ranch near Ottine and what he believed would be the safety of his amigo Martin Robledo's home.

According to Américo Paredes, in his book *With His Pistol in His Hand,* Gregorio arrived at the Robledo place sometime around sundown. The first thing he did was kick off his shoes and give his tired, abused feet a sorely needed rest. During the forty or so hours he punished those poor blister covered doggies, one of the men chasing him actually came up with a workable plan for catching Cortez Lira—brutal but workable.

Gonzales County Sheriff Robert M. Glover had been a very close personal friend of the recently departed Brack Morris. When Bob got word of his bosom compadre's unfortunate death at the hands of a gun toting Mexican peon, he almost burst a blood vessel in his head gathering a posse, getting to a horse, and pounding it for Karnes City. But somewhere along the path he had a flash of lawman genius. Why bother chasing around all over the country for this pistol packing tamale when there were people who knew exactly where to find him? It's rumored still that this stunning flash of intelligence came about an hour or so after Sheriff Bob and his party of deputies stopped at several well-known watering holes along the way and downed a few dippers of Old Tarantula Killer. Just a little fortifier to kind of get the blood flowing, don't you know.

Well by the time Glover arrived in Karnes City, Gregorio's mother, wife, sister-in-law, and wounded brother had all been rounded up and thrown in the seediest cells of the local hoosegow. Gonzales County's determined sheriff is said to have applied some "pressure" to one of the incarcerated women. She resisted at first but eventually relented and gave him Martin Robledo's name and where he could be found. Who got "pressured" and how is still not known, but if later events were any indication, the method probably wasn't pretty and was very likely brutal in the extreme. Glover and his bunch made up all the ground lost to the fire-footed Gregorio by boarding a train for Ottine and then riding the hell out of some good horses.

Martin Robledo, his wife, Refugia, their three sons, another young man—Ramón Rodríguez—who lived with them, and a close friend named Martin Sandoval had welcomed Gregorio into the Robledo home, fed him, and listened intently to his hair-raising story. As they all relaxed on the front porch, the discussion turned to how they would handle the situation if the *rinches* (Texas Rangers) showed up. Everyone enthusiastically agreed that they should, and would, most definitely fight. Well, it didn't take long for that decision to be put to the bloody test.

At the very moment Gregorio came out on the Robledos' porch and shucked his shoes to give his toes a little wiggle in the cool evening air, Bob Glover and his eight-man posse took up assault positions in the scrubby brush behind the house. Indications are that everyone passed the bottle, took another snort of Old Overcoat, and got ready for a fight with what they believed was the largest and most heavily armed band of Mexican banditos any of them had ever faced. Just how much stump juice got poured down their collective gullets is still open to conjecture. But anyone trying to use what happened next as proof of sober judgment ought to have his face slapped till his ears ring like cathedral bells.

Everyone in the posse dismounted except Glover. The plan was for all the deputies to rush the house from a variety of directions as the still mounted sheriff charged in from the front.

Gruesome scene of typical justice meted out to Mexican "bandits" along the Texas-Mexico border during the late 19th century. It was just such methods that put Gregorio Cortez to running for the safety of Mexico after he killed two Texas lawmen. (Photo courtesy of Western History Collections, University of Oklahoma Libraries)

But something went wrong. As an inflamed Bob Glover approached the house near the corner of the porch where Gregorio sat wiggling his toes, the shooting commenced before everyone in the posse managed to get in place and prepare for action.

The lawmen swore the blasting started when someone in the house fired first. Whether true or not, most everyone did manage to agree later that Glover and Cortez traded the initial shots and continued their exchange until the surprised sheriff tumbled off his horse as dead as his recently buried friend, Brack Morris.

Chapter 6

Then all hell broke loose. In the darkness and confusion people started running in every direction. The only way this could be put on film would be to resurrect Abbott and Costello and have it played out like a scene from their motion picture about meeting Frankenstein and the Wolf Man at the same time. One of the deputies managed to stop loping around in the dark long enough to fire through a window and blast the hell out of an unarmed Ramón Rodríguez. Screaming people ran back and forth in every room of the house, deputies sprinted around trees, through bushes, and into horses while pouring lead into anything and everything, moving or not.

Refugia, Robledo's wife, tried to keep her three youngest sons from being killed by hovering over them and got plugged for her troubles. Someone standing close to posse member Henry Schnabel—aforementioned owner of the ranch Martin Robledo rented—blew away half his head with a blast that left powder burns on the skin of what was left. Various posse members reported vicious close quarter, hand-to-hand battles with hordes of ruthless Mexican killers. Local newspapers carried stories afterward proclaiming it a God sent miracle *all* the lawmen weren't slaughtered in the ferocious battle.

Eventually the shooting died down, and when everything got tallied up, there were two dead Texas lawmen and a wounded woman and teenage boy. Most of the Robledo family was "captured," but that wasn't near the end of the evening's fun and games. As reported in the *San Antonio Express*, thirteen-year-old Encarnación Robledo got the brunt of the remaining posse members' rage. They wanted to know where the rest of the Cortez gang would run to hide, so they hung him from a tree limb till his face turned blue and his tongue jutted out of his mouth. The fact that the thirteen-year-old child knew nothing to tell didn't seem to put a damper on the "let's hang him till his eyeballs pop out" party. For the hangers this was absolute proof that the hangee and all his associates were indeed a desperate bunch who would rather die than talk.

The posse then rushed the prisoner family to San Antonio in an effort to keep them from being lynched by the irate—and of course grossly misinformed—citizens of Gonzales. Señora Robledo, who had no weapon at the time and tried valiantly to save her children by throwing her own body in the line of fire from the posse, was charged with the murder of Henry Schnable. A deputy named Harper, who swore he saw her shoot at the dead man from a window, claimed that he had gallantly defended Schnable when the man fell near him with half his head blown off.

Señora Robledo never faced a jury on that scurrilous charge. Harper later changed his story and ended up facing unproven allegations that he was responsible for accidentally shooting Schnable in the head during the Battle of Belmont's insanity and confusion.

To reinforce their horse-feathered windy-whizzer of a story, posse members claimed to have found an arsenal of weapons comprised of ten Winchester rifles and a bucket full of loose cartridges. A month later when hearings finally started, the number of weapons had dwindled from ten to eight and finally got down to a lone Winchester rifle and a single-barreled shotgun, which was about what you could have expected to find in any household in Texas at the time. Not only that, but testimony from one of the deputies who had been on the scene indicated that, in his opinion, neither of the weapons had been fired that night.

As soon as Sheriff Glover bit the dust that deadly evening, Gregorio Cortez jumped off the porch, barefooted, and ran straight into a piece of ground covered with those nasty little Texas grass burrs. When he realized that his shoes still sat on the Robledos' front porch, he sat down, ripped his vest apart,

South Texas cowboys such as those shown here made up the greater part of the posses that chased Gregorio Cortez Lira all over South Texas. They had little luck catching him. (Photo courtesy of Western History Collections, University of Oklahoma Libraries)

wrapped his feet with the tattered rags, and hid in a field not far from the house. After the gunfire and commotion finally stopped, he slipped back to the Robledos', found his shoes, and headed south as fast as his sore feet could take him.

About ten miles into the newest leg of his flight, he came to the banks of the Guadalupe River and the home of his close friend Ceferino Flores. Flores supplied his fugitive amigo with another sorrel mare and a saddle and traded his pistol for the one Gregorio had taken from the body of Sheriff Morris.

A posse following a pack of bloodhounds chased Gregorio into the waters of the Guadalupe before they dropped the effort and went back to Ceferino's place to give him a taste of the old Encarnación Robledo treatment. They didn't get much in the way of information from him either, but Flores eventually ended up spending two years in the Texas state calaboose for trying to help a desperate friend.

Between Saturday morning June 15 and late Sunday evening, Gregorio Cortez rode Ceferino Flores' sorrel mare from the Guadalupe to the San Antonio River. If he had been able to travel in a straight line, the trip would have only covered about fifty miles. But between the doubling back, laying false trails, and circling around those in pursuit, he probably traveled at least three times that. At about six o'clock Sunday night, the mare dropped dead near Floresville.

Gregorio took the saddle and bridle, eluded his pursuers, and found another mare in a field on the outskirts of town. His run from Floresville to Cotulla—a distance of about a hundred miles—ended up covering about three hundred miles because of all the necessary evasive maneuvers. Every time the posse members thought they were just about to catch the wily criminal, the brown mare sprinted away, leaving the dumbfounded lawmen standing in the dust scratching their heads. According to the Paredes' version of the story, at least six of the posse members' horses died from the brutally punishing chase.

Hundreds of men representing every county and municipality he passed through or near joined in on the hunt. Cortez would lose one determined group of worn-out trackers only to be confronted with a new and fresh bunch just as he thought he had managed to get away.

Eventually it became apparent to those chasing him that their prey was headed for Laredo. Men and horses were loaded onto special trains that traveled back and forth on the Corpus Christi to Laredo railroad. Every time someone spotted him, the posse, along with its horses and dogs, was rushed to the site to take up the chase. As soon as they lost the trail again, everyone and everything got loaded back on the train for much-needed food and rest until Gregorio made a mistake and once more got spotted. Then they did the whole song and dance all over again. It's the same method the Pinkerton Detective

Chapter 6

Agency used to run Butch Cassidy and the Sundance Kid out of the country.

The skill and gritty toughness of man and animal so amazed all those who pursued Cortez that the *San Antonio Express* voiced the opinion that the only way to catch the clever criminal involved calling out all the able-bodied men in the country and filling every open piece of ground in South Texas with the body of an armed guard to close off all possible arteries of escape.

One of his favorite tricks to throw his hunters off the track was to stop, go around in circles for a bit, reverse direction, cross back through the circle and then jump to a grassy spot. Some of the best trackers in Texas lost hours trying to pick their way though that clever piece of business. He stayed in the bush when possible, cut fences, used herds of cattle to cover his tracks, and in one instance got so thirsty and desperate that he drove a small herd up to a water hole guarded by posse members who mistook him for a vaquero who worked on a neighboring ranch.

Eventually Gregorio's brown mare caved in too. She managed to cut one of her hind legs jumping over some barbed wire, and he had to abandon her in a thicket near Cotulla. A posse so close he could hear them breathing sent out word that it had, for the umpteenth time, cornered the most dangerous desperado in Texas but had to retract that statement the next day when they discovered that Cortez had slipped through their fingers again. Not only did he get away, he baffled them all again by heading directly into Cotulla, home of most of the men who made up the posse.

What they didn't know and would only discover after his capture, was that when the little brown mare cashed in her chips, she took most of his will to continue. He later admitted to his captors that by that point the lack of food, water, and sleep had so sapped his energy that he totally gave up the ghost and waited for any one of the various posses chasing him to catch up and place him under arrest. But no one showed up, and after a nice little rest he managed to recuperate enough to go on. He rolled the dice again, because the Rio Grande and the safety of Mexico weren't that far away.

In broad daylight, Gregorio walked out of his hiding place and marched into Cotulla like any other field hand on a trip to town. It fooled the gringos but not the other Mexicans he met along the way. A friendly señora provided him with some food and water around noon on June 20 and then he headed for the Nueces where a number of armed men guarded the bridge across the river. Instead of trying to walk over the bridge, he followed the shallow stream till he was underneath the wooden span, took a bath, and then swam to the other side where he stretched out in the shade for a little siesta before striking out for the town of Twohig. By the time he got to that tiny village, his exhaustion caught up with him again and he was forced to lie down for another nap—a nap that lasted a day and a half.

On June 22, which was his twenty-sixth birthday, the some-what refreshed outlaw walked into the village of El Sauz where he bought some new clothes and changed what little American currency he possessed into Mexican pesos. At that point it was only about thirty miles to the Rio Grande, freedom, and safety. His plan was to blend in with all the other laborers in the area and simply walk into Mexico with a group that crossed back and forth pretty much anytime they wanted during that period. Unfortunately his fantastic string of luck had run its course.

Around noon on June 22, Jesús González, a man familiar with and who immediately recognized Gregorio Cortez, spotted the fugitive as he entered the sheep ranch of Abrán de la Garza. By that point just about everyone in South Texas was aware of a $1,000 reward offered by the governor to anyone who could aid in the capture and conviction of Texas's most sought-after criminal. González beat a hot path over to a group of Texas Rangers led by Captain John H. Rogers camped only two hundred yards from Garza's sheep ranch. Gregorio Cortez had barely taken a seat for a little badly needed *almuerzo* when Rogers and posseman K.H. Merrem stepped up and placed him under arrest.

It was all so anticlimactic. This unknown Mexican corn farmer had killed two Texas sheriffs in blistering gun battles, and for ten days damn near every gringo in Texas had chased the resourceful killer all over the south central part of the state. Some had even exchanged gunfire with him. He had made them all look foolish and managed to cover an estimated one hundred twenty miles on foot and put more than four hundred miles on the sorrel and brown mares. Hundreds of deputized and undeputized men had joined in the search, but when the last line got written, it only took one Texas Ranger and a civilian assistant to capture him. At least that's how the most widely accepted version of the story goes. Several others exist, but for our purposes we'll stay with the one you just read.

It would be putting it mildly to say that the Mexican population of the area was upset with Jesús González for betraying the man they now viewed as a local legend and heroic figure. Most felt him a traitor, and in the end the gringos of Karnes City managed to figure out a way to cheat him out of the bulk of the reward money. When it all finally shook out, González only collected about two hundred dollars for betraying a man who had considered him a friend.

Gregorio Cortez Lira was put on trial a number of times. His initial hearing started on July 24, 1901, and the jury hung eleven to one for conviction on the charge of first-degree murder in the death Henry Schnabel. This has to be viewed as a curious turn of events given that he probably had absolutely nothing to do with Schnabel's unfortunate departure. But

Noted Mexican bandit and killer of several Texas lawmen, Gregorio Cortez Lira is shown here seated between two of his captors outside the Bexar County Jail. (Photo courtesy of Western History Collections, University of Oklahoma Libraries)

prosecutors had wrung a fantastic statement out of Señora Robledo that alleged she had seen Cortez kill Sheriff Glover on the east side of her house and then run to the west side and blow half of Schnabel's head off. In return for this ridiculous assertion the charge that she had killed Schnabel was, of course, dropped. Eventually the jurors worked out a deal, and they sentenced Cortez to prison for fifty years for second-degree murder.

Nobody came away from the trial pleased with the verdict. Cortez pitched a fit when the decision was read in court. Some said he used "strong" language to give vent to his anger with the outcome. His lawyers filed motions for a new trial, and the judge unceremoniously denied them. The *Express* carried a story that quoted sheriffs and deputies who had virtually filled the courtroom expecting Cortez to hang as being "very disappointed."

Worst of all, about a week after the trial ended, Romaldo Cortez died in the Karnes City jail. His wound had been horrendous, but the family maintained that he was recovering and was able to walk around his cell and talk with visitors only a few days after being shot. Nonetheless he "unexpectedly" passed away while still in custody, and there wasn't a damned thing anyone could do about it.

A few days after Romaldo's death, a mob of Karnes County church deacons, civic leaders, and temperance advocates estimated at between 300 and 350, tried to break into the Gonzales jail and drag Gregorio out for a little Texas necktie party. But a conscientious sheriff with a lot of hard bark on his backside named F. M. Fly kept that particular miscarriage of justice from happening.

Six months later, in January 1902, logic finally reared its head and the Texas Court of Criminal Appeals threw the Gonzales verdict out. In their opinion Gregorio Cortez, although a remarkable man, could not have been in two places at the same time. What a concept! Prior to the rendering of that verdict, Gregorio was moved to Karnes City, put on trial for the murder of Sheriff Brack Morris, and quickly sentenced to death.

No attempts at lynching the prisoner were made during the Morris hearing. The omnipresent sheriffs decided to allow justice to take its due course and only resort to mob righteousness as an alternative if the decision went against them again. Much to their collective disappointment, the Court of Criminal Appeals reversed the Karnes City verdict and also the Pleasanton judgment rendered after a fast and furious trial found Gregorio guilty of horse theft.

A Goliad jury couldn't come to an agreement when he was retried for the murder of Sheriff Morris. The charges were dismissed, and it all ended up in Corpus Christi where it was tried once again April 25-30 in 1904. That jury found him not guilty, but in the meantime he'd been convicted of the murder of Sheriff Glover and, when he lost that one on appeal, wound up in the Texas State Penitentiary in Huntsville on January 1, 1905.

The legal wrangling in his various prosecutions had lasted almost four years. When Gregorio finally entered Huntsville, he had already served time in eleven jails in eleven different counties of Texas and had not seen a single minute's worth of bonded freedom. During the course of all this life-rending upheaval, Cortez and his wife, Leonor, divorced. Her father testified at the Goliad trial that the defendant and his daughter were no longer married and that as a consequence she tended to be "prejudiced against her former husband."

The now famous bandito was married a second time on December 23, 1904, while in the Columbus jail awaiting transfer to Huntsville. His new bride, Estéfana Garza, and several other women who claimed to have been his sweethearts at some point before all the notoriety, appeared during that same time. Former lovers and potential wives seemed to pop up everywhere like honey-filled sopapillas. Evidently the handsome twenty-six-year-old Gregorio had managed to spread his affections all over South Texas.

His Anglo jailers' attitudes toward their famed Mexican prisoner changed dramatically over the period of his incarceration while his fate was decided during the state's numerous trials. County Sheriff Bridge even arranged for Gregorio's second marriage. It was performed by a local judge and witnessed by a number of other county officials. The accommodating sheriff even went so far as to arrange for the whole second floor of his jail to be used as a honeymoon suite from the day the love-birds were married till Gregorio left for Huntsville a week later.

Upon arrival at the penitentiary, he gave his occupation as barber, and prison officials allowed him to work at that trade during his entire stay with them. His even-tempered affability, an innate skill at making friends of his keepers, and an ability to adapt to any given situation went a long way to explaining the notation on his prison certificate of conduct that read, "Occupation, barber; habits, temperate; education, limited."

From the moment he set foot in prison on January 1, 1905, the efforts to obtain his release started. They persisted unabated until July 14, 1913, when thirty-eight-year-old Gregorio Cortez Lira signed his acceptance of a pardon granted by then Governor O.B. Colquitt. Altogether he had served twelve years in jail or prison—almost one third of his life—for making the mistake of doing a little routine horse-trading.

Naturally the popular reaction to his release ran the gamut of emotions. The Mexican community universally approved of the pardon while their Anglo counterparts seemed to be all over the map with their attitudes and sentiments. This dichotomy was probably best exemplified by the differences in editorial comment found in the two newspapers in Beeville. The *Beeville Picayune* simply reprinted an article from the *Laredo Times* followed by a brief and relatively impartial account of the events surrounding the entire unfortunate affair. The *Beeville Bee* pitched an editorial hissy fit with an article entitled "Dangerous Murderer Pardoned."

Cortez headed for Nuevo Laredo where he got himself involved in the Mexican Revolution on the side of the Huertistas. At some point he was badly wounded and might have also been captured only to escape just before his planned execution. At any rate he returned to Manor, Texas, and lived with his son Valeriano while he recuperated from his wounds.

Once his health had improved sufficiently, he moved to Anson where he was married for a third time early in 1916. The name of that wife is not known for certain. Some feel she might have been a woman named Esther Martínez who lived nearby in the town of Big Spring.

Shortly after the wedding he complained of sudden pain, became ill, and abruptly died. The Américo Paredes account of the incident quotes Valeriano Cortez as having believed that his father was the victim of a poisoning. The *New Handbook of Texas* claims that he got sick and passed away from the effects of pneumonia. From the available descriptions of his death, the most probable cause of his exit was a heart attack. Gregorio had led an extremely hard and violent life. Death at forty-one in such a manner should not have been all that unexpected. His burial took place in a little cemetery a few miles outside Anson, five hundred miles from the border where he was born and the places that made him famous.

As has been the case with many folk heroes, the physical passing of Gregorio Cortez inspired a variety of stories about the events surrounding his adventures. Most popular of those were the various *corridos,* or ballads, that began appearing as early as 1901. The best known of them was called *El Corrido de Gregorio Cortez*. Over the passing years interest in the story has waxed and waned arriving at a pinnacle in 1982 with the popular motion picture version of his life, *The Ballad of Gregorio Cortez*, that starred actor Edward James Olmos.

Afterword

I have every confidence that there will be those overwhelmed with the need to second-guess your esteemed scribbler and grouse over the selection of those men included for examination in this volume. Visitors to my table during previous book signings of *Texas Bad Girls* have proven to me that everyone seems to have his or her favorite when it comes to those who practiced the outlaw or murder trade.

In many instances the person touted is a well-known local bad dude who terrorized the folks around Aledo for years. Or an infamous bad girl who ran a home for wayward cowboys that everyone in Ponder knew about and hey, you mean you've never heard of Horizontal Hattie or Albino Bob Matoose?

Ladies who want to debate the definition of hussy are among my favorite quibblers. They're usually around my grandmother Rachel's age and just a huge hoot to talk with about what they deem *bad*. So by way of clarification, please know that the chapter on Watt Moorman was the result of an extensive search for someone whose name did not come easily to the lips of dabblers in Texas history when asked to identify a well-known Texas killer of the early nineteenth century.

Ol' bushwhacking Watt had just begun to take literary shape when my friend Mackey Murdock walked up one night at the DFW Writer's Workshop and said, "Have you ever heard of a guy named Curg Border?" (Go back and read that question at half speed and at an octave lower level that sounds like you're talking from the bottom of a barrel, and you'll have a stellar imitation of Mackey down pat.) Well, of course, Curg Border was a total question mark, and his place in these pages was immediately assured.

As was mentioned in the foreword, John Wesley Hardin had to appear given his place in the heavens of psychotic behavior and possible serial murderer status. The man professed in his own autobiography to have killed over fifty people. The thing you have to remember is that he didn't necessarily count those of African American extraction or Mexicans as men. So the actual total number of murders he committed could have been as much as twice that figure.

Killin' Jim Miller was a shoo-in to appear for the absolute cold-bloodedness of his actions and the fact that the number of those who departed this life at his hands could very well have rivaled Hardin's figures. And Pink Higgins, while not nearly as prolific as either Hardin or Miller, admitted to at least eleven killings and given his rather ambiguous reference to his actions, might well have been responsible for a few more than that.

Gregorio Cortez Lira didn't come anywhere close to accomplishing the number of murders his Anglo counterparts could claim and safely carve into their pistol grips. But during his brief ride for freedom, he managed to create more in the way of public interest in his singular deeds and their aftermath than anyone who came before him, or anyone who came afterward for a good many years. His was a special story that needs to be retold every so often to remind us in the most graphic terms how deadly events can unfold based exclusively on a simple misunderstanding. His status as one of Texas's baddest boys is based not simply on the two dead men he left behind, but also because of the tumultuous events inspired by those deaths. Not one of the other bad men covered in these pages can boast of causing such universal upheaval over so broad an area in so short a time. His actions and societal responses to them were, beyond any doubt, simply amazing.

Murder and criminal activity of any other sort is for the most part disgusting on its very face. Dragging the crimes committed by these men into the light of day and rehashing the events surrounding them should never be interpreted by the reader as an effort to somehow make killers like John Wesley Hardin look better or add to their infamous reputations. The effort here should never be interpreted as trying to portray them as picturesque or appealing. The humor derived from the retelling of their life stories was always done in an attempt to have a little fun with history and should never be taken as making fun at the expense of anyone in particular.

Bibliography

Askins, Charles. *Texans, Guns & History.* New York: Winchester Press, 1970.

Burton, Arthur T. *Black, Red, and Deadly.* Austin: Eakin Publications, Inc., 1991.

Blake, James Carlos. *The Pistoleer.* New York: Berkley Books, 1995.

Butts, J. Lee. *Texas Bad Girls: Hussies, Harlots, and Horse Thieves.* Plano, TX: Republic of Texas Press, 2000.

Cain, Del. *Lawmen of the Old West: The Good Guys.* Plano, TX: Republic of Texas Press, 2000.

_____. *Lawmen of the Old West: The Bad Guys.* Plano, TX: Republic of Texas Press, 2001.

Cannon, Bill. *A Treasury of Texas Trivia.* Plano, TX: Republic of Texas Press, 1997.

Chariton, Wallace O. *This Dog'll Hunt: An Entertaining Texas Dictionary.* Plano, TX: Wordware Publishing, Inc., 1989.

Clancy, Paul, et al. "Booming Business for Boomtown Gamblers." *The Old West: The Gamblers.* Alexandria, VA: Time-Life Books, Inc., 1975.

Combs, Joe F. *Gunsmoke in the Redlands.* San Antonio: The Naylor Company, 1968.

Cunningham, Eugene. *Triggernometry: A Gallery of Gunfighters.* Norman: University of Oklahoma Press, 1996.

Cuthbertson, Gilbert M. "Regulator-Moderator War." *New Handbook of Texas.* Austin: Texas State Historical Association, 1996.

Bibliography

Cox, Patrick. "Thompson, Ben." *New Handbook of Texas.* Austin: Texas State Historical Association, 1996.

Douglas, C.L. *Famous Texas Feuds.* Dallas: The Turner Company, 1936.

Eckhardt, C.F. *Tales of Bad Men, Bad Women and Bad Places: Four Centuries of Texas Outlawry.* Lubbock, TX: Texas Tech University Press, 1999.

Fehrenbach, T.R. *Lone Star: A History of Texas and the Texans.* New York: The Macmillan Company, 1968.

Fricke, Michael Moorman. "Moorman, Charles Watt." *New Handbook of Texas.* Austin: Texas State Historical Association, 1996.

Haggard, John V. "Neutral Ground." *New Handbook of Texas.* Austin: Texas State Historical Association, 1996.

Hall, Terry. *Cowboy Wisdom: Proverbs, Advice, Lore, Yarns and Lies.* New York: Warner Books, 1995.

Hardin, John Wesley. *The Life of John Wesley Hardin: As Written by Himself.* Norman: University of Oklahoma Press, 1961.

Harkey, Dee. *Mean as Hell.* Santa Fe: Ancient City Press, 1989.

James, Bill C. *Jim Miller: The Untold Story of a Texas Badman.* Wolf City, B.C. James, 1983.

Jameson, W.C. *Bubba Speak: Texas Folk Sayings.* Plano, TX: Republic of Texas Press, 1998.

_____. *Unsolved Mysteries of the Old West.* Plano, TX: Republic of Texas Press, 1999.

Jent, Steven A. *A Browser's Book of Texas History.* Plano, TX: Republic of Texas Press, 2000.

Metz, Leon C. *El Paso Chronicles: A Record of Historical Events in El Paso, Texas.* El Paso: Mangan Books, 1993.

_____. "Hardin, John Wesley." *New Handbook of Texas.* Austin: Texas State Historical Association, 1996.

_____. *John Wesley Hardin: Dark Angel of Texas.* Norman: University of Oklahoma Press, 1996.

_____. *The Shooters.* El Paso: Mangan Books, 1976.

Moulton, Candy. *The Writer's Guide to Everyday Life in the Wild West.* Cincinnati: Reader's Digest Books, 1999.

Nolan, Frederich. *Portraits of the West.* London: Salamander Books Limited, 1997.

O'Neal, Bill. *Encyclopedia of Western Gunfighters.* Norman: University of Oklahoma Press, 1979.

_____. *The Bloody Legacy of Pink Higgins.* Austin: Eakin Press, 1999.

Orozco, Cynthia. "Cortez Lira, Gregorio." *New Handbook of Texas.* Austin: Texas State Historical Association, 1996.

Paredes, Américo. *With His Pistol In His Hand.* Austin: University of Texas Press, 1998.

Potter, Edgar R. *Cowboy Slang.* Phoenix: Golden West Publishers, 1986.

Rafferty, Terrence. "See No Evil." *Gentlemen's Quarterly.* New York: GQ Incorporated, October 1999.

Robinson III, Charles M. *The Men Who Wear the Star: The Story of the Texas Rangers.* New York: Random House Press, 2000.

Rosa, Joseph G. *The Gunfighter: Man or Myth?* Norman: University of Oklahoma Press, 1969.

_____. *The Taming of the West and the Age of the Gunfighter.* New York: Smithmark Publishers, Inc., 1993.

Selcer, Richard F. *Hell's Half Acre: The Life and Legend of a Red-Light District.* Fort Worth, TX: Texas Christian University Press, 1991.

Bibliography

Shirley, Glenn. *Shotgun for Hire: The Story of "Deacon" Jim Miller, Killer of Pat Garrett.* Norman: University of Oklahoma Press, 1970.

Sonnichsen, C.L. "Allison, Robert Clay." *New Handbook of Texas.* Austin: Texas State Historical Association, 1996.

_____. "Horrell-Higgins Feud." *New Handbook of Texas.* Austin: Texas State Historical Association, 1996.

_____. *I'll Die Before I'll Run.* Lincoln: University of Nebraska Press, 1988.

_____. *10 Texas Feuds.* Albuquerque: University of New Mexico Press, 1957, 1971, 2000.

Trachtman, Paul. "Sinister masters of murder." *The Old West: The Gunfighters.* Alexandria, VA: Time-Life Books, Inc., 1975.

Wheeler, Keith. "A pride of literary lions." *The Old West: The Chroniclers.* Alexandria, VA: Time-Life Books, Inc., 1975.

Woods, Larry J. "Gunfighters and Lawmen." *Wild West.* Leesburg, VA: PRIMEDIA Enthusiast Group, August 2000.

Index

Index

Index

Also by J. Lee Butts:

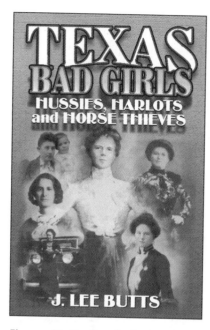

Texas Bad Girls: Hussies, Harlots, and Horse Thieves

J. Lee Butts

All the gossip, scandal, secrets, and wild behavior of every well-known bad girl that ever stepped over the state line is told in this hilarious book. Author Butts also introduces us to the hijinks of some lesser known but not better behaved women. He covers the bad girls masquerading as "ladies" as well as some you'd rather not run into at the end of a dark street. Butts' wicked sense of humor comes through on every page.

Jimmy Butts lives in Irving, Texas, with his wife. He retired to become a full-time writer because he says he will not work for corporate America ever again. No matter what.

1-55622-833-3 • $17.95 US / $27.95 CAN.
248 pp. • 5½ x 8½ • paper

Looking for more?

Check out these and other great titles from Republic of Texas Press

Lawmen of the Old West: The Bad Guys

Del Cain

1-55622-834-1 • $18.95
240 pages • 5½ x 8½ • paper

Lawmen of the Old West: The Good Guys

Del Cain

1-55622-677-2 • $16.95
232 pages • 5½ x 8½ • paper

Texas Ranger Tales II

Mike Cox

1-55622-640-3 • $18.95
296 pages • 5½ x 8½ • paper

Texas Ranger Johnny Klevenhagen

Douglas V. Meed

1-55622-793-0 • $18.95
248 pages • 5½ x 8½ • paper

Last of the Old-Time Texans

Mackey Murdock

1-55622-784-1 • $17.95
248 pages • 5½ x 8½ • paper

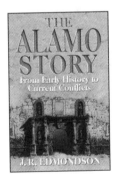

The Alamo Story
From Early History to Current Conflicts

J.R. Edmondson

1-55622-678-0 • $24.95
446 pages • 6 x 9 • paper